FLOYD D. BEACHUM AND CARLOS R. MCCRAY

cultural collision and collusion

reflections on hip-hop culture, values, and schools

PETER LANG
New York • Washington, D.C./Baltimore • Bern
Frankfurt • Berlin • Brussels • Vienna • Oxford

Library of Congress Cataloging-in-Publication Data

Beachum, Floyd D.
Cultural collision and collusion: reflections on hip-hop culture,
values, and schools / Floyd D. Beachum, Carlos R. McCray.
p. cm. — (Educational psychology: critical pedagogical perspectives; v. 14)
Includes bibliographical references and index.
1. African Americans—Education. 2. Multicultural education—United States.
3. Education, Urban—United States. 4. Critical pedagogy—United States.
5. Hip-hop. I. McCray, Carlos R. II. Title.
LC2717.B43   371.829′96073—dc22   2010014251
ISBN 978-1-4331-0594-4
ISSN 1943-8109

Bibliographic information published by **Die Deutsche Nationalbibliothek**.
Die Deutsche Nationalbibliothek lists this publication in the "Deutsche
Nationalbibliografie"; detailed bibliographic data is available
on the Internet at http://dnb.d-nb.de/.

FSC
Mixed Sources
Product group from well-managed
forests, controlled sources and
recycled wood or fiber
Cert no. SCS-COC-002464
www.fsc.org
©1996 Forest Stewardship Council

The paper in this book meets the guidelines for permanence and durability
of the Committee on Production Guidelines for Book Longevity
of the Council of Library Resources.

In Loving Memory of

Flordia L. Beachum

Learde Smith

Dr. Asa Hilliard, III

Contents

Foreword

As we conclude the first decade of the 21st century, our nation finds itself in the midst of an educational crisis. The forces of neo-liberalism have transformed public schools into tradable commodities that privilege market values over engaged democratic citizenship. Progressive curriculum and pedagogy are being supplanted by the "teach to the test" strategies that are implicitly demanded by *No Child Left Behind* and other technocratic policy initiatives. Despite growing levels of surveillance and militarism, our schools are increasingly vulnerable to crime and violence.

For Black youth, the current moment is even more desperate. A range of draconian public policies from anti-baggy pants legislation to civil injunctions against gangs mark a full-fledged war against Black youth. Escalating rates of joblessness, poverty, homelessness, gun violence, and other indices of social misery continue to undermine the life chances and educational futures of our children. Within schools, Black students are underrepresented among graduation cohorts and overrepresented in special education classrooms, suspension rolls, and dropout statistics. It is in the midst of these tragic and urgent circumstances that many scholars, critics, and everyday citizens scramble for illuminating theories and transformative solutions.

Unfortunately, much of the current discourse on African Americans and schooling continues to ignore deeply entrenched structural impediments to educational and social prosperity. From the representations of messianic leadership in popular school films like *Freedom Writers* to the resurgence of "individual responsibility" rhetoric by both Democratic and Republican politicians, the overestimation of individual action continues to obscure the persistent forces of inequality that over-determine social realities. Such a posture not only promotes an unhelpful structure of Manichaeism, but also forecloses on possibilities for more nuanced and careful inquiry into social problems.

Within mainstream liberal intellectual circles, the excessive focus on individualism frequently leads to a kind of analytic tunnel vision that concedes the existence of inequality, but places exclusive focus on the suffering side of the equation. As a result, we continue to pose questions that are indispensable but ultimately inadequate for deep interrogation of social problems. Rather than figuring out how and why certain police "patrol while racist," which would force us to examine the ways that whiteness functions as an agent of symbolic and physical violence, we resign ourselves to probing the consequences of "driving while black." Instead of studying "the school funding gap," which would force us to make sense of differential investments in educational futures along lines of race, class, and geography; scholars have focused on the so-called "achievement gap," which places the efforts and outcomes of Black and Brown youth under the light of scrutiny. Such distinctions are not merely rhetorical, but index a circumscription of our modes and methods of understanding the social world.

In this book, Floyd Beachum and Carlos McCray attempt to push our thinking forward by offering a more complex assessment of the conditions faced by African American youth in contemporary schooling contexts. Rather than merely asking, "Why are Black children struggling?" they spotlight the complex social, cultural, and political forces that frustrate the efforts of Black children who navigate the rough waters of today's schools. Underpinning their analysis are two provocative concepts, "cultural collision" and "cultural collusion," both of which lend much needed analytic texture to the current conversations on Black youth and schooling.

The first term, cultural collision, builds on decades of theoretical and empirical work within the broad tradition of progressive education scholarship. This vast body of work, which draws from sociology, anthropology, psychology, and a range of educational subfields, has persuasively demonstrated how schooling contexts clearly operate in ways that are culturally-specific, yet are consistently marked and negotiated as though universal. Such insights are critical for spotlighting the ways that minority school failure is often linked to disconnects between the in-school and out-of-school lives of students rather than biological, moral, or cultural defects. Beachum and McCray add layers of insight to this important literature through their sharp analysis of the current cultural, political, and economic moment.

At the center of this book's understanding of cultural collision is a sophisticated and nuanced understanding of hip-hop culture. Rather than reducing hip-hop to a body of contentious rap music texts, the authors rightly acknowledge the complex of rituals, codes, ideologies, and aesthetics that give hip-hop culture its distinctive character and cultural integrity. Their work builds on the current literature of hip-hop based education by moving beyond curricular interventions and close textual readings, and demonstrating how the cultural logic of hip-hop informs student behavior, attitudes, and expectations within the schooling context. It is from this posture that Beachum and McCray are able to offer a historically and culturally specific analysis of the particular "collisions" that often mark Black youth's negotiation of school, as well as provide concrete suggestions and solutions for bridging the current cultural gaps.

The other provocative concept raised in this book is "cultural collusion," which Beachum and McCray use in reference to the ways that educational leaders participate in the marginalization and ultimate elimination of Black youth within schools. Through their examination of how falsely obvious deficit narratives about Black youth permeate the porous cultural boundaries of schools, we are better positioned to understand how educators, even those who are well intentioned, become complicit in the assignment of lowered expectations, unnecessarily punitive discipline, and unmerited blame to Black students. Such insight is not only valuable to the research literature, but serves as an important point of reference for teacher education, professional development, youth mentoring, and community activism.

This book is a timely and necessary contribution to the current literature on Black youth and schooling. Unlike many books of its kind, it does not force us to choose between critique and responsibility, theory and practice, or hope and pragmatism. Instead, it demands that we muster all of our intellectual, emotional, and spiritual resources and use them in the service of justice and prosperity. If we remain committed to the spirit of this text, we just may see the change for which we have struggled.

MARC LAMONT HILL
TEACHERS COLLEGE, COLUMBIA UNIVERSITY

Preface

Cultural Collision and Collusion: Reflections on Hip-Hop Culture, Values, and Schools represents a shift in the paradigm of educational literature. In order to understand our meaning by this, it is appropriate to explain what this book is not. This book is not a commentary on the so-called pathological nature of students in urban areas. It is not a deepening of deficit-minded literature that once again over-blames blighted communities, parents, and students. Nor is it another text that replicates a long line of well-documented research on the existence and nature of structural inequalities (though we agree with this literature). Finally, it is not another book overly invested in cultural differences, even though culture is a primary theme throughout the text.

Rather, this work acknowledges the social history, policies, values, and practices that have placed urban schools and many others in less than optimal situations. In addition, teachers, administrators, and others who deal with students on a daily basis are coping with phenomena that are not readily examined in contemporary research literature. This work seeks to explore another side of the issue regarding students in the urban context in a way that acknowledges the broader framework, but at the same time examines the reactions, behaviors, and choices that evolve from that context. Thus, *Cultural Collision and Collusion* becomes our means to this end. This book represents the compilation of related works on the aforementioned subjects over the last seven years.

• The purpose of this book is to (a) broaden the scholarly dialogue, (b) examine and disseminate relevant research to practitioners, and (c) address the complexity and problems around youth culture and school culture, especially in urban areas. This work seeks to provide insight into youth culture and some manifestations of popular culture (e.g., hip-hop). In addition, it will examine some of the tensions that develop when the values of youth and adults collide in U.S. schools. Finally, we intend to utilize the extant literature for insight and enlightenment in the best interest of academic inquiry and practical applicability. The practical reality for far too many urban schools is one that reflects the despair, dire socioeconomic situations, and a complex cultural ethos of numerous neighborhoods and countless youth. Thus, a more rigorous analysis and critical appreciation of youth is necessary because their issues are complex, multifaceted, and delve deeper than what we might see on television or hear in trite or superficial conversation. This context creates quite a daunting situation for educational leadership in not only urban schools, but all schools.

The information in this work will also focus on multiple educational disciplines, although the most immediate implications may be best suited for educational psychology. The overall knowledge base will be enhanced due to the educational interdisciplinary approach. Ergo, it has additional implications for educational leadership, curriculum and instruction, educational policy, and urban education (to name a few). The multidimensional nature of our approach gives the work the freedom to highlight multiple and diverse voices while at the same time provides a forum for different (and sometimes divergent) methodologies, philosophies, and ideologies.

The motivation for the exploration of notions of cultural collision and collusion originated years ago when co-author Floyd D. Beachum was in Milwaukee, WI. On September 29, 2002, a group of youth (including a ten year old), attacked and beat 36-year old Charlie Young to death in an inner-city Milwaukee neighborhood. The Milwaukee Journal Sentinel reported the following:

A mob of nearly 20 kids beat a man brain dead Sunday night after he confront-ed them for throwing an egg at him and punched one teen in the mouth, police said.

Eight suspects, at least one as young as 10, were in custody Tuesday, police said. The victim, Charlie Young Jr., 36, remained on life support.

Police said the group chased Young onto the porch of a house at 2021 N. 21st Lane and used bats, shovels and boards to pummel him in an attack that left blood splattered floor to ceiling.

At one point, Young forced his way into the lower unit in a desperate bid for safety, the landlord said, but the kids dragged him back outside, where the beat-ing continued until police responded to a neighbor's 911 call.

The severity of the attack demonstrated an escalating problem that plagued the area near Johnsons Park all summer, shaken neighbors say: out-of-control teenagers who roam the streets intimidating residents [sic].

Police say the attack occurred around 10:30 p.m. Sunday after Young chased a small group after the egg was thrown. He caught a 14-year-old boy and punched him in the mouth, knocking out a tooth, police said.

The juveniles quickly assembled a larger group of 18 or 20 kids ranging in age from 10 to 18 and chased Young to the porch. Police say the mob then beat the man with shovels, boards, sticks and bats.

Although this is an extreme case it does underscore the complex array of issues in urban communities. However, this work remains current as the nation reels from the shock of the recent beating death of an honor roll student in Chicago. These issues include concentrated poverty, vio-lence, lack of police presence, drugs, gang proliferation and influence, and community apathy and powerlessness (to name a few). These same issues inevitably carry over into schools. Thus, a line of questioning began to develop around the lives of young people in urban schools. At the same time, it seemed as if hip-hop was the soundtrack to the streets and was a subtle subtext. Many hip-hop songs that resonated with many urban Black youth seemed to glorify materialism, violence, and misogyny, but obviously these problems were not created by hip-hop music. In addition, hip-hop has now emerged into a cultural phenom-enon now including clothing, dialects, energy drinks, websites, reality

TV shows, books and magazines, and even video games. Therefore, the measure of the past (looking solely at rap music) is no longer valid; culture is much too dynamic.

Ultimately, what was needed was a more encompassing way to theorize the complex intersections of issues in the lives of youth in urban schools. We (the authors) began to examine the literature at the time only to find that there was not much research to be found on urban schools, youth, and hip-hop culture. Two very insightful works at the time were *Race Rules: Navigating the Color Line* by Michael Eric Dyson (1997) and *The Hip Hop Generation: Young Blacks and the Crisis in African American Culture* by Bakari Kitwana (2002). The Dyson book contains a chapter entitled, "We never were what we used to be: Black youth, pop culture, and the politics of nostalgia." In this chapter, Dyson takes a critical look at how adults and the media view Black youth and hip-hop culture. He recounts how nostalgia makes the older generation believe that their memories, experiences, and music are superior to the younger generation. He further denotes the seductive, yet faulty logic this promotes. Every generation must be viewed in context and in relationship to the world in which they live. Thus we cannot expect the hip-hop generation to be the civil rights or black power generation, but we can expect them to learn the lessons and appreciate the struggles which have given them the opportunity to enjoy contemporary privileges not even imagined a couple of generations ago. As we examine the lives of 21st century youth and their educative experiences, we should keep these lessons in mind. The book by Bakari Kitwana discusses the generation of people who came after the civil rights generation, largely raised with hip-hop. They have lived long enough to see its birth, expansion, and growing pains. Kitwana also describes the unique problems this generation faces: unemployment (not to mention outsourcing of jobs), policing and incarceration, relationship troubles between the sexes, activism, politics, and the generational divide (civil rights generation vs. hip-hop generation). These works (among others listed in this book) provided foundational knowledge, crucial context, and a broader understanding.

The debate surrounding the plight of urban areas and their residents has been the subject of much study and preoccupation. Alas, many of these debates have become dichotomized into extremely opposite poles. On the one end, there are those who believe that urban dwellers (especially ones in poverty) themselves are the cause of their own plight due to their own lack of effort, bad decisions, and/or deviant culture (i.e., they have not pulled themselves up by their bootstraps). The opposing view asserts that urban residents are the victims of larger structural or environmental variables such as racial/ethnic discrimination, policies, politics, and/or historical practices to name a few. One must wonder who bears the responsibility for change? We recognize the multifaceted, complex nature of many blighted urban areas in the United States. Cultural and structural issues are intertwined and we all have an ultimate responsibility to foster positive change on an individual level and a collective/societal level. We need diverse groups to collaborate across confining lines of race/ethnicity, social class, gender identity, ability status, etc. thereby forging a new solidarity, or as we argue in the last chapter, if not a new solidarity then an insurgency.

This book adds the additional variable of hip-hop culture which forces concerned adults to engage youth in what can sometimes be unfamiliar and strange territory. And as we commit to this work, we must keep in mind that hip-hop culture may need the same philosophical lens that we apply to the structural/cultural debate. As educators, we should promote and model good manners, restraint, patience, and effective decision-making. This could help our youth as they clarify and cultivate their own value systems. In the places where hip-hop culture encourages negativity, we provide a different reality or alternative viewpoint. At the same time, educators should work to change regressive policies, commit to community service, volunteer on critical decision-making committees (within and outside of education), and even run for certain elected offices. All of the aforementioned suggestions are aimed at impacting broader structural issues.

The first time cultural collision (as applied to education) appeared in the literature was in a chapter in an edited book titled, *Sex, Race, Ethnicity, and Education*, published in 1976. The chapter was written by Dr. Russell H. Coward Jr. In his chapter he discussed the conflict between White educators (teachers and administrators) and Black students in urban schools. At the time, there was massive white flight to the suburbs accompanied by increasing Black populations migrating to inner cities.

This was the essence of his conception of cultural collision. Although our work is very different with regard to time and context, there are some similarities with regard to addressing the alienation and segregation of urban communities and encouraging educators to have an affirming (as opposed to deficit) view of urban school students. In light of our subject matter, we find it necessary to highlight his work.

With this book we hope to begin a more thoughtful conversation in reference to urban youth, schooling, and hip-hop culture. Academically, we endeavor to stretch the knowledge base to include more scholarly research on these topics. Practically, we see the need to produce work that more accurately reflects what teachers, administrators, and educational service providers are dealing with on a daily basis in their schools. We should all keep in mind the words of Mary McCleod Bethume, who stated:

> We have a powerful potential in our youth, and we must have the courage to change old ideas and practices so that we may direct their power toward good ends.

FLOYD D. BEACHUM

CARLOS R. McCRAY

Acknowledgments

I would like to first thank several special family members beginning with my loving and supportive wife, Katerri. To my son Devin, your dreams can come true if you have patience, persistence, and a plan. I would like to thank my mother, Mattie, educator, wisdom-giver, and friend. I would also like to thank the Beachum, Suggs, Oates, Brewer, Stacks, James, and Mumford families for assisting in my growth or touching my life. To the Puryear, Bush, Redmond, Simmons, and Olison families, thank you for welcoming me and my family into yours. Your support and love have been a blessing to us.

In the academy I would like to acknowledge the following organizations: ACPSI (Africana Cultures and Policy Studies Institute), BOTA (Brothers of the Academy), and LASER (Linking Academic Scholars to Educational Resources). I would like to thank all of my colleagues at the University of Wisconsin-Milwaukee, especially in the Department of Administrative Leadership. Thanks for giving me my start. I would also like to thank all of my colleagues in the College of Education at Lehigh University. We do not operate as islands and no one makes it alone; therefore I would like to thank the following people who I consider mentors: Drs. Na'im Akbar, Michael E. Dantley, James E. Davis, Ira Bogotch,

Fenwick English, and Linda Tillman. I would like to give special thanks to a towering scholar who mentors, teaches, and writes emphasizing equity and high quality, Dr. Festus E. Obiakor.

I have had the pleasure of meeting several good friends on my life journey. Some of these include: Ares Smith, Roosevelt Mosley, Cedric L. Rembert, Clifford Mustaafa Dozier, and last but not least a great thinker, scholar, and colleague, Carlos R. Mccray. Thanks to all mentioned and apologies to anyone I may have forgotten.

FLOYD D. BEACHUM

First and foremost, I would like to acknowledge my parents Willie and Joyce McCray. I would like to thank them for their guidance and support throughout my years. It is through their guidance and support that I am able to continue to do great things. This book is only one testament to the impact that they have had and will continue to have on my life. I would also like to thank Tesia Love, whose intellectual conversation motivated me to write a little more. There were also many times in which I simply wanted to hear from good friends and relatives to talk about sports as I completed the book. Thus, I would like to thank Marion Smith, Jr., LTC Cecil Copeland III, Derrick Bryant, Kelvin Wright, and Maj. Jibraun A. Emerson, for their constant belief in me and making those phone calls to simply say "what's up…Did you see the game this weekend?" Those phone calls meant more than they know. Finally, I would like to thank all of my aunts, uncles, and cousins for their guidance over the years, helping to make me the person I am today.

I would like to acknowledge two of my mentors and friends, Dr. Michael E. Dantley, the Associate Vice Provost and Vice President of Academic Affairs at Miami University, and Dr. Linda Tillman, Professor at the University of North Carolina at Chapel Hill. These two individuals have had a tremendous impact on my career in the academe. They have always been there for me and were always willing to share their advice and opinions. Linda has been a great confidant and mentor. Michael has not only been a great confidant and mentor, but he also has helped tremendously in cultivating my skills as a writer. I am very grateful to Michael for all the trips he and Floyd made to Atlanta in an effort to finish a great special issue for the *Journal of School Leadership*. It was Michael's mentoring and encouragement that gave me the inspiration and hope to believe that such an endeavor of this magnitude was possible. I would also like to thank all of my colleagues at Fordham University for their inspiration. Finally, I would like to submit a special thank you to Dr. Hayward Richardson of Georgia State University who served willing and sometimes unwilling as a sounding board and constructive critic in the completion of this project.

CARLOS R. MCCRAY

We would also like to thank the following:

ORGANIZATIONS:

AERA (American Educational Research Association)
UCEA (University Council for Educational Administration)

COLLEAGUES AROUND THE COUNTRY:

Greg Goodman, Michelle Young, Jeffery Brooks, Khaula Murtadha, Maria Gonzalez, Catherine Marshall, Gary Crow, Catherine Lugg, James Koschoreck, James Scheurich, Mark Gooden, Gerardo Lopez, Mariela Rodriguez, Patrick Pauken, Judy Alston, Eugene Sanders, Audrey Dentith, Gerald Cattaro, Bruce Cooper, Sheldon Marcus, Tobi Tetenbaum, Chance Lewis, Carolyn Brown, Jerlando Jackson, Kathleen Cashin, James Moore, Lamont Flowers, Juan Gilbert, John Lee, Marvin Lynn, Rene Antrop-Gonzalez, Thankdeka Chapman, Raji Swaminathan, Edgar Epps, Stanley, Kaminsky, Marty Sapp, Brenda Townsend, Gwendolyn Webb-Johnson, Monika Shealey, Wanda Blanchett, Beverly Cross, Dorothy Autrey-Harris, Allen Stewart, James V. Wright, Clarence Thomas, and Lisa Chavers.

We would also like to give a special thanks to Gary Dillon for his hard work in helping us find a cover for the book. Gary is pursuing his doctorate at Fordham University.

Chapter One

Through the Fire

How Pretext Impacts the Context of African American Educational Experiences

> We have a powerful potential in our youth, and we must have the courage to change old ideas and practices so that we may direct their power toward good ends.
>
> —MARY MCLEOD BETHUNE

The above quote is a challenge to all who are concerned about the plight of today's youth. The former portion of the statement affirms the ability of Black youth to take the reins of destiny and chart a course into the future. The latter part of the quote challenges us to reexamine what we have been doing and in many cases change the way we think and act for the betterment of students. Across the U.S., from politicians and public officials to students and parents, people are calling for reform, restructure, and change in schools. In response, the federal government, over the years, began to emphasize higher graduation rates, accountability, more standardized testing, more rigor in academic subjects, and educational excellence (Obiakor & Beachum, 2005b). The pressure placed on schools for educational excellence can promote a paradigm or paradigms based on technical efficiency, empiricism, scientific rationalism, and modernism (Dantley, 2002; Giroux, 1997). Thus, it is assumed that the best way to improve schools is by raising test scores on standardized tests (quantitative data), the promotion of *cookie-cutter*, recipe-style, linear models, and an ideology that treats all students and communities as equals, when equity is what is needed.

To complicate matters, the 21st century has witnessed the explosion of technology, entertainment, and popular culture. Gause (2005a) asked a series of relevant questions regarding popular culture and education:

> How are schools and educational leaders keeping up with this global transformation? What type of impact does this transformation of schools from sites of democracy to "bedfellows" of consumerism have upon the school and much larger global community? How are the 'souls' of schools affected? (p. 242)

These poignant questions propose significant challenges for today's educators. While trying to survive day-to-day providing students with a quality education, they must also deal with outside pressures from the national, state, and local levels. Concurrently, they must also prepare students for a future that is sure to be marked by technological advancement, the necessity of innovation, increased conceptual capacity, and the need to deal with people of different cultures, creeds, and characters (Nisbett, 2009).

Cultural collision is a clash in beliefs, cultures, or values (see Beachum & McCray, 2008). For the purposes of our discussion, we emphasize the clash in cultures between youth (primarily youth of color in urban contexts) with the culture of educators and systems of education. A different, yet related, concept is cultural collusion, which can be described as "the negative cultural/societal implications that emerge when complex cultural cues and messages seem to influence individual and group behavior" (Beachum & McCray, 2008, p. 104). This collusion specifically identifies "highly visible youth cultures, in this case violence, materialism, misogyny, and hip-hop culture" (Beachum & McCray, 2008, p. 104).

In order to grasp the contemporary impact and outcomes of cultural collision and collusion, one must understand how these concepts originated and evolved. This chapter's organization is informed by the insightful work of French sociologist Loic Wacquant (2002) who proposed "not one but several 'peculiar institutions' have successively operated to define, confine, and control African-Americans in the history of the United States" (p. 42). These peculiar institutions are as follows: (1) Slavery (1619–1865); (2) Jim Crow/Segregation (1865–1965); (3) Ghetto (1915–1968); (4) Hyperghetto and Prison (1968–today). Using this framework, we will discuss historical highlights of the time period (what was happening), Blacks' attitudes toward education and shared cultural values at the time, and contradictions and complexities that caused unification or division, harmony or disagreement, and shifts in how Blacks saw themselves and the world.

Nobody Knows the Trouble I've Seen: The Scourge of Slavery

Historical Context

Slavery in the United States of America remains a painful part of the nation's history. Its psychological, economic, and educational impacts are still being felt to this day (Akbar, 1984; Kunjufu, 1995). Thompson III (2007) described this institution as follows:

> Although the U.S. has been described as a melting pot of various cultures, European capitalistic values and traditions have dominated this mix since its inception, long supplanting the theocratic system imported to North America by the early settlers. The opportunity to make huge profits in the New World led colonial entrepreneurs to use any means necessary to exploit the vast untapped resources of their recently claimed land. This included using force to extract labor from unwilling participants. After a trial-and-error period with Native American and indentured European workers, the 'perfect' labor force for this harrowing task was identified on the African continent. Subsequently large numbers of Africans were brutally uprooted and shipped like cargo to strange lands hundreds of miles across the sea. (p. 50)

This quote encapsulates some of the purposes and processes regarding American slavery. Therefore, this peculiar institution promised huge profits through a massive system of forced labor. The process of obtaining this labor force meant the inhumane capture of human bodies and transporting them from one continent to another. This process would be rife with physical and psychological terror (Beachum, Dentith, & McCray, 2004; Perry, 2003). Blassingame (1979) gives yet another scathing summary:

> The chains of the American Negro's captivity were forged in Africa. Prince and peasant, merchant and agriculturalist, warrior and priest, Africans were drawn into the vortex of the Atlantic slave trade and funneled into the sugar fields, the swampy rice lands, or the cotton and tobacco plantations of the New World. The process of enslavement was almost unbelievably painful and bewildering for the Africans. Completely cut off from their native land, they were frightened by the artifacts of the white man's civilization and terrified by his cruelty until they learned that they were only expected to work for him as they had been accustomed to doing in their native land. Still, some were so remorseful they committed suicide; others refused to learn the customs of whites and held on to the memory of the African cultural determinants of their own status. (pp. 3–4)

It is quite evident and well-documented that that slavery was an evolutionary industry that employed physical and psychic terror for the purposes of financial gain and the solidification of racial supremacy. It is also important to note that even in the midst of overwhelming and impossible odds, the Africans rebelled, resisted, sought ways to keep cultural traditions, and most of all reaffirmed their own humanity and forged ahead with the hope of a brighter day.

Educational Attitudes

The enslaved Africans in the U.S. were certainly discouraged from learning (except for maybe the most basic information). "Law and custom made it a crime for enslaved men and women to learn or teach others to read and write" (Perry, 2003, p. 13). Once again, against these laws and customs, enslaved Africans still made attempts to become literate. The tactics used to discourage the slaves were horrific; this was countered by ingenious strategies employed by slaves in order to learn. Perry (2003) wrote:

> There are the stories of slaves who were hanged when they were discovered reading, and of patrollers who went around breaking up Sunday meetings where slaves were being taught to read, beating all of the adults who were pre-

sent. Slaves cajoled white children into teaching them, trading marbles, and candy for reading lessons. They paid large sums of money to poor white people for reading lessons and were always on the lookout for time with the blue black speller (a school dictionary), or for an occasion to learn from their masters and mistresses without their knowing. (p. 13)

Here we see the desire and passion for education among slaves. At some point during slavery, slaves became aware of the importance of becoming literate (Perry, 2003). They realized the great power and potential in being educated and what it meant for changing their status. This struggle by enslaved Africans to become educated occurred against an entrenched social system that constantly reinforced the slaves' subordinate status, hopeless plight, and so-called intellectual incapability or inferiority. Interestingly, many slave owners believed that education would "spoil" a slave gave making them discontented instead of docile (Douglass, 1968). Thompson III (2007) gives additional insight into the mentality of many Whites who supported slavery when he stated, "An educated slave was commonly viewed as dangerous and a direct contradiction to the slavery philosophy" (p. 57). Ultimately, the educational endeavor was much larger than an individualistic pursuit (even though there were obvious personal benefits); what we see is the building of a foundation to launch future freedom struggles. Education would play a critical role in not only attaining physical freedom; it also had the potential to liberate slaves from their psychological chains. In addition, education was viewed as something to be shared with the community. Again, Perry (2003) asserted:

While learning to read was an individual achievement, it was fundamentally a communal act. For the slaves, literacy affirmed not only their individual freedom but also the freedom of their people. Becoming literate obliged one to teach others. Learning and teaching were two sides of the same coin, part of the same moment. Literacy was not something you kept for yourself; it was to be passed on to others, to the community. Literacy was something to share. (p. 14)

At the same time, we also see that education was not for education's sake; *education was synonymous with liberation* (Beachum et al., 2004). This theme would guide the slaves who would eventually be called African Americans in their long journey to freedom and beyond.

Complexities and Contradictions

Indeed, the Africans faced insurmountable odds and a bleak existence in the U.S. Somehow, they maintained the high value of education, family cohesiveness, language patterns, and song. It is rather ironic that the slaves were portrayed to be intellectually inferior to Whites, but Africa was home to renowned educational institutions. "During the early 1500s, Sankore was a renowned intellectual center to which scholars from all over Africa, Asia, and Europe came to study" (Thompson III, 2007, p. 57). Thus, the negative stereotyping and false imagery was clearly manufactured to support the institution of slavery (Akbar, 1984) and a dehumanization of all Africans. Africans placed a high value on family even amid the scourge of slavery. It was commonplace for slaves to be separated and sold to far off plantations by way of slave auctions (Blassingame, 1979). In many cases, fictive kinship relationships developed where another slave would become a surrogate family member. This was very important because the family proved to be an "important survival mechanism" against slavery (Blassingame, 1979, p. 191). Even though traditional African languages and dialects would slowly change to English, slaves kept their traditional cultures alive by infusing them into English. "Regardless of his previous culture, upon landing in the New World the African-born slave had to learn the language of his master. Taught by overseers or native-born slaves, the African acquired a few European words in a relatively casual and haphazard fashion" (Blassingame, 1979, p. 24) in order to perform tasks and to engage in minimal communication. The slaves retained a special reverence for spirituality, even as Christianity slowly replaced African religions. Similarly, music and dance also played a critical role not only in the lives of enslaved Africans, but also in the lives of Africans in the American diaspora.

Music is more than an avenue for entertainment only. For the slaves, it was integrated into their lives. In this particular time period, spirituals told the collective story of struggle. Stuckey (1987) wrote:

> Too often the spirituals are studied apart from their natural, ceremonial context. The tendency has been to treat them as a musical form unrelated to dance

and certainly unrelated to particular configurations of dance and dance rhythm...That the spirituals were sung in the circle guaranteed the continuing focus of the ancestors and elders as the Christian faith answered to African religious imperatives. (p. 27)

Here we find that spirituals incorporated dance and collaboration (together in a circle) with multiple purposes (emphasis on Christian faith and African traditions). Blassingame (1979) summarized the focus and intent of spirituals when he stated:

The sentiments of the slave often appear in the spirituals. Songs of sorrow and hope, of agony and joy, of resignation and rebellion, the spirituals were the unique creations of the black slaves. Since, however, the spirituals were derivations from Biblical lore and served as a means of intra-group expression in a hostile environment, they naturally contain a few explicit references to slavery...Even when slaves did model their songs on those of whites, they changed them radically. (p. 137)

From this quote we learn that spirituals were uniquely created by the slaves and even when they adopted the songs of Whites, they changed the songs to better reflect their experiences. The really important concept to note here is that through this form of musical expression, slaves told a story, their story, and by collectively engaging in this activity it was shared with succeeding generations. Here we find that music can be more than simply an expression of art, it can be intricately intertwined with one's life. We will return to this theme later.

In sum, slavery was a dark period for Blacks in this country. Although it had an economic intent, it also reinforced notions of Black ignorance, inferiority, and incapability. Thus, the initial experiences of far too many Blacks in this nation were tainted by this peculiar institution. At the same time, the slaves still struggled to become literate, support family, maintain their culture (language, dance, and spirituals), and ultimately resign themselves to survive in the hope for a brighter tomorrow. Unfortunately, the next phase was not that bright as slavery gave way to segregation.

I've been in the Storm too long:
Jim Crow/Segregation

Historical Context

Eventually, slavery was totally abolished in the North while it somewhat intensified in the South. The American West would become contentious territory as the question of would slavery expand to newly admitted states arose. At the same time, the competing economic goals of the industrial North and the agricultural South slowly guided the two large factions of our country into a bloody Civil War, with the status and future of Blacks at the epicenter. The American Civil War ended with the defeat of the South and the collapse of slavery as a formal institution. A short period of relative progress called Reconstruction (1865–1877) occurred in which many former slaves attained voting rights, began to attain a formal education, and, for the first time in the U.S., saw a glimmer of hope in the darkness. This glimmer was quickly squelched as the Northern armies that provided protection and maintained order in the South pulled out. The result was a new era which could be termed Jim Crow or segregation.

Jim Crow laws were largely enforced in the South, while the North did have its forms of racism, segregation became law in Southern U.S. states. These laws were marked by the intentional separation of races (i.e., White and Black). Woodward (1974) asserted that these codes "extended to churches and schools, to housing and jobs, to eating and drinking. Whether by law or by custom, that ostracism extended to virtually all forms of public transportation, to sports and recreations, to hospitals, orphanages, prisons, and asylums, and ultimately to funeral homes, morgues, and cemeteries" (p. 7). The newly freed slaves posed a two-fold threat to the Southern social regime. First, the slaves being freed meant the immediate end to a massive free labor force and now the potential competition with Whites for jobs. Second, the new status of Blacks posed a significant threat to the system of deference, dehumanization, and racial superiority that Southern Whites had depended on for so long (Wacquant, 2001). Part of segregation's function would be to deal with both issues, "Under this regime, backed by custom and elaborate legal statutes, superexploitative sharecropping arrangements and debt peonage fixed black labor on the land, perpetuating the hegemony of the region's agrarian upper class" (Wacquant, 2001, p. 101). At the same time, "segregation laws sharply curtailed social contacts between whites and blacks by relegating the latter to separate residential districts and to the reserved 'colored' section of commercial establishments and public facilities, saloons and movie houses, parks and beaches, trolleys and buses, waiting rooms and bathrooms" (Wacquant, 2001, p. 101). These laws were supported not only by White communities, but also by local police regimes. This allowed for the growth and expansion for domestic terrorist groups like the Ku Klux Klan. What this also meant was Blacks could not rely on the police or local/state legal systems for protection, therefore they were vulnerable, (West, 2004). Woodward (1974) observed, "Indeed the more defenseless, disfranchised, and intimidated the Negro became the more prone he was to the ruthless aggression of mobs" (p. 87). Although segregation was a harsh reality, Blacks created nurturing communities and endeavored to educate children and instill in them a sense of pride.

Educational Attitudes

An interesting phenomenon occurred amid the ever-imposing environment of segregation. Instead of segregation totally devastating the educational aspirations of Blacks, in many cases, it actually strengthened their spirits and resolve. Segregation not only regulated the physical movement of Blacks, but it also took a psychological toll on them as well (Perry, 2003; Thompson III, 2007). Schools were of course segregated, and although they were separate they were certainly not equal (even though separate but equal was the law at this time). In fact, "in many areas Negro schools were disgracefully behind schools for whites" (Woodward, 1974, p. 145). What these schools lacked in facilities and resources, they made up for in attitude and determination. While the dominant Southern social order suggested to Blacks that they were nobody (almost subhuman), schools and communities reinforced the refrain "be somebody." This meant to "be a human, to be a person, to be counted, to be the opposite of a slave, to be free" (Perry, 2003, p. 26).

Obtaining an education was the key to being somebody. Similarly, schools during this time period not only provided academic preparation to Black students, but they also prepared them for the world beyond the schoolhouse doors (including the world of segregation and Jim Crow). The academic focus was supplemented or grounded in a pedagogy that purposely cultivated student self-esteem. Another example of this would be the *110 rule*. Many educators would tell their students that 100 percent was not good enough; you had to strive for 110 percent (Kunjufu, 2002). Schools in the segregated South with effective and caring Black educators in many cases promoted academic excellence and personal mastery. In sum, Perry (2003) insightfully asserted:

> There was a systematic denial and limiting of educational opportunity for African Americans precisely because they were African Americans. The philosophy of education that developed was informed by the particular ways in which literacy and education were implicated in the oppression of African Americans. It informed the role that education and schooling would assume in resistance and the struggle for freedom from the time of slavery to the Civil Rights era. (p. 51)

The philosophy here was one that viewed education as a process and product of liberation.

Complexities and Contradictions

Although it seems rather easy to totally indict the South in its determined focus on establishing and enforcing a system of segregation, it is easy to overlook the contradictory attitudes in the North. Woodward (1974) insightfully wrote, "One of the strangest things about the career of Jim Crow was that the system was born in the North and reached an advanced age before moving to the South in force" (p. 17). Although Blacks in the North did enjoy certain freedoms, such as more freedom of movement and more freedom to challenge overt forms of racism, these freedoms existed in a context of White superiority and Black inferiority. Again Woodward noted:

> For all that, the Northern Negro was made painfully and constantly aware that he lived in a society dedicated to the doctrine of white supremacy and Negro

inferiority. The major political parties, whatever their devotion to slavery, vied with each other in their devotion to this doctrine, and extremely few politicians of importance dared to question them. Their constituencies firmly believed that the Negroes were incapable of being assimilated politically, socially, or physically into white society. They made sure in numerous ways that the Negro understood his 'place' and that he was severely confined to it. (p. 18)

Although this quote is primarily describing the North around the end of slavery, it is evident that such attitudes continued well past slavery's demise (Woodward, 1974). A glaring example of Northern apathy toward the newly freed Blacks is seen in the Compromise of 1877. After the American Civil War, Northern armies in the South played a key role in maintaining order while Southern resentment, outrage, and vengeance boiled beneath the surface. This compromise that on the one hand made Rutherford B. Hayes president of the U.S., on the other guaranteed the abandonment of Blacks in the South. Although some Southern politicians pledged to protect the rights of Blacks, they soon became empty rhetoric. "But as these pledges were forgotten or violated and the South veered toward proscription and extremism, Northern opinion shifted to the right, keeping pace with the South, conceding point, after point, so that at no time were the sections very far apart on race policy" (Woodward, 1974, p. 70). As White America's attitudes toward Blacks became more apathetic, Blacks found other ways to cope with the backlash. Music became one of the avenues of freedom by means of self-expression.

Music can provide unique insight into the souls of a people. Perry (2003) wrote, "To know what a people believes, one should of course pay attention to what they say, what they portray in music, poetry, and stories" (p. 27). This particular time period was marked by forms of musical expression such as gospel and blues. What we know now as gospel music grew out of the same cultural crucible as slave spirituals. In this era, Blacks now could meet in their own churches and openly worship in their own unique ways. "African American gospel represents the flip side of the blues. Spirituals are a powerful emotional testimonial to the depths of despair, atonement, and redemption, juxtaposed with an unshakeable faith that God will ultimately prevail" (White & Cones, 1999, p. 55). We discover the deep connection to spirituality here along with the belief that a brighter day was ahead. In addition, Blacks found a way to communicate and pass on a shared history and collection of experiences while acknowledging something greater than oneself. The blues, on the other hand, was a different form of musical expression.

The blues also told the story of Blacks, but in a different way than gospel. "The bluesman articulates the pain and suffering in a pattern of African-American speech and images that the listener who has lived the Black experience can understand" (White & Cones, 1999, p. 55). Here again, musical expression is not divorced from the everyday lived experiences of Blacks. It tells of struggle, strife, pity, problems, reality, and resilience. In this way, the blues was more than an impotent outlet for entertainment only; it became a way to communicate the shared cultural set of experiences complete with musical accompaniment. West (2004) wrote:

> As infectious and embracing as the blues is, we should never forget that the blues was born out of the crucible of slavery and its vicious legacy, that it expresses the determination of a people to assert their human value. The blues professes to the deep psychic and material pains inflicted on black people within the sphere of a mythological land of opportunity...The patient resilience expressed in the blues flows from the sustained resistance to ugly forms of racist domination, and from the forging of indistinguishable hope in the contexts of American social death and soul murder. The blues produced a mature spiritual and communal strength. (p. 93)

Once again, music reinforced a set of values such as spirituality, community, self-expression, self-reflection, and the undying commitment against forms of oppression in that day and time.

What's Going On? The Urban Ghetto

Historical Context

The time period from approximately 1915 to 1968 encompasses a large portion of the 20th century. This period would witness events such as two world wars, the Great Depression, and a momentous struggle to end segregation culminating in the American Civil Rights movement. During the first part of the century, segregation was still alive and well. Along with segregation came an era of physical and psychological terror for Blacks as evidenced by brutal lynching, beatings, harassment, and verbal abuse (Thompson III, 2007; Woodward, 1974). Wacquant (2000) summarized the plight of Blacks at the time, writing:

> The sheer brutality of caste oppression in the South, the decline of cotton agriculture due to floods and the boll weevil, and the pressing shortage of labor in northern factories caused by the outbreak of the First World War created the impetus for African-Americans to emigrate en masse to the booming industrial centers of the Midwest and Northeast (over 1.5 million left in 1910–30, followed by another 3 million in 1940–60). But as migrants from Mississippi to the Carolinas flocked to the northern metropolis, what they discovered there was not the 'promised land' of equality and full citizenship but another system of racial enclosure, the ghetto, which, though it was less rigid and fearsome than the one they had fled, was no less encompassing and constricting. (pp. 4–5)

Thus, the North promised a new beginning devoid of the obvious racial barriers that were prevalent in the South. Ironically, while offering a new life, the North also offered new forms of segregation as Blacks were ushered into certain segments of Northern cities which came to be known as ghettoes.

The 20th century witnessed the migration of masses of Blacks to the industrial North from the agricultural South. According to Jackson (1996), "From 1915 to the 1930s, 1.8 million Southern Blacks migrated to industrial cities in the North and Midwest" (p. 234). Villegas and Lucas (2002) noted, "In 1940, for instance, almost 80 percent of the African American population lived in the South, and 63 percent lived in rural areas; thirty years later, only 33 percent lived in the South, and 75 percent lived in urban settings" (p. 46). It was the hope of many to find better job opportunities, to escape the segregation and violence in the South, and to possibly gain access to a small slice of the "American Dream." Unfortunately, life in the North provided only minimal opportunities and a more nuanced and covert form of racism as compared to the South. Rothstein (1996) agreed, "Wherever they went however, they found the pernicious segregation system. This affected where they went to school, where they worked, and the type of employment they were able to obtain" (p. 163). This would eventually lead to a phenomenon which would increase the "geographic isolation" of people of color from their White counterparts, called *White flight*. White flight would be the next event in a chain that would isolate urban dwellers (mainly of color) and their schools.

Educational Attitudes

Whites in many urban areas began to leave as the number of Blacks (and other people of color) increased. They escaped to suburbs away from the cities, leaving a void. This process became known as "White flight." Malcolm Gladwell (2000) borrows this term in his book *The Tipping Point: How Little Things Can Make a Big Difference*; he opined:

> The expression [Tipping Point] first came into popular use in the 1970s to describe the flight to the suburbs of whites living in the older cities of the American Northeast. When the number of incoming African Americans in a particular neighborhood reached a certain point—20 percent say—sociologists observed that the community would 'tip': most of the remaining whites would leave almost immediately. (p. 12)

This quote expresses the core attitude against racial integration. The result would be exceedingly different schools: "The suburbanization of the United States has created two racially segregated and economically unequal systems of education—one urban, mostly for children who are poor and of color; the other suburban, largely White, middle-class children" (Villegas & Lucas, 2002, p. 48). This process would have detrimental effects on communities and schools of color in the inner cities. Blacks who moved to the North found a more nuanced, less overt, yet equally if not more damaging form of oppression. The experience in the industrial North gave the façade of limitless opportunities (which were actually very limited) while also making transparent a harsh reality, which included isolation, neglect, and an inferior infrastructure for schooling.

Blacks would try their best to hold on to their deep belief in education as a means of liberation. This philosophy was now challenged by the harsh reality of urban life. While isolated in segregated parts of major cities, crime rates began to increase, businesses began to leave, and the meaning of community for Blacks began to wane.

Complexities and Contradictions

During this time period Blacks faced numerous challenges. In the South, segregation was still the rule of the day, undergirded by the terrorist tactics of groups like the Ku Klux Klan. By the mid-20th century, serious resistance to segregation began to mount. A watershed moment occurred with the *Brown v. Board of Education* (1954) decision.

> The landmark Supreme Court decision in the *Brown v. Board of Education* case has been hailed as the single most important court decision in American educational history. The decision in this case overturned the *Plessey v. Ferguson* separate but equal clause by establishing that segregated schools denied African American students their constitutional rights guaranteed to them in the 14th Amendment. *Brown*...would also serve as the impetus for challenging several inequities as Jim Crow laws in the South and, on a many levels, for generally protecting the civil rights of African Americans and later individuals with disabilities. (Blanchett, Mumford, & Beachum, 2005, p. 70)

While this movement impacted the physical manifestations of oppression, in conjunction, the Black Power movement started to deal with how Black people felt about themselves, by instilling self-reliance, self-sufficiency, and in some cases self-protection. Similarly, White and Cones (1999) wrote:

> At a deeper, more personal level, it was about the right of self-determination and self-definition. The Reverend Martin Luther King, Jr. used terms like "somebodyness" to define the psychological meaning of the revolution. Other terms coined to reinforce this concept were "Black pride," "Black is Beautiful," and "Black Power"...self-definition from the perspective of one's own experience is the first step in deconstructing the oppressor's negative definitions. (p. 63)

As Blacks strived to dismantle oppressive laws (i.e., Jim Crow) and deal with the psychological effects of ongoing mistreatment, music remained a means of dealing with reality as well as expressing their innermost feelings.

During this time period jazz as well as rhythm and blues (R&B) became popular. Jazz has been hailed a musical form that characterizes imagination and invention. West (2004) wrote, "These great blues and jazz musicians are eloquent connoisseurs of individuality in their improvisational arts and experimental lives" (p. 91). Dyson (1997) characterized jazz as "...its heart pumping with the blood of improvisation, its gut churning with the blues—embody the edifying quest for romantic self-expression and democratic collaboration that capture Negro music and American democracy at their best" (p. 126). With its emphasis on improvisation, individuality, and expression, jazz represented yet another form of music that transcended the boundaries of mere entertainment-laden titillation. According to West (2004), jazz was much more, "The blues and jazz made it possible to engage race in America on personal and intimate terms—with democratic results" (p. 92). West (2008) provided even more clarity when he wrote:

> What is jazz all about? It's about finding your voice. It's about that long, difficult walk to freedom. It's about mustering the courage to think critically. It's about mustering the courage to care and love, and be empathetic and compassionate...Jazz is the middle road between invisibility and anger. It is where self-confident creativity resides. (p. 118)

Thus, in the early to mid-20th century, jazz provided Blacks a unique form of musical expression in the midst of Southern segregation and Northern isolation.

The 1960s and early 1970s clearly represented a unique time period for Blacks. Dyson (2007) agrees, "In the 1960s and 1970s, black folk were struggling for the sorts of political freedoms and economic opportunities that the most fortunate members of the young black generation now take for granted" (p. 63). The movement toward Black liberation was supported by music that began to reflect the struggle. At this time you also had the Black Arts Movement (BAM). "For the members of the Black Arts Movement, there was no such thing as a serious artist who was not concerned about the struggles for self-determination and political liberty of their people, struggles which in large part inspired their art" (Dyson, 2007, p. 62). So when one hears Curtis Mayfield's "Keep on Pushin,'" James Brown's "I'm Black and I'm Proud," or Sam Cooke's, "Change Is Gonna Come," these works cannot easily be separated from the times in which these artists lived. In sum, music can be utilized strictly for entertainment value, but for Blacks, it has historically served a greater purpose. "Music has been our most powerful creative expression. Of course, the music itself is based on communal links of church, family, and social education. Our music reflects our unique sense of rhythm, harmony, and melody" (West, 2008, p. 114).

Get Rich or Die Tryin': The Hyperghetto/Hood and 21st Century Black America

Historical Context

The last 40 years have brought even more changes to the world and to Blacks. The final institution that Wacquant proposed was the hyperghetto. Once again, his framework explains how the four institutions "operated to define, confine, and control African-Americans in the history of the United States" (Wacquant, 2000, p. 377). Our utilization of his framework in this chapter is to provide a historical model to better understand the historical, educational, and sociocultural experiences of Blacks in the U.S. The hyperghetto evolved in a post-White flight era when the residential barriers that barred Blacks from moving into White suburbs were relaxed (Wilson, 2009). Thus, White flight was followed by *Black trek* as more Blacks with greater wealth left inner-city communities leaving a dangerous void in what was the ghetto (Dyson, 2004). In addition to the spatial separation, Wacquant (2001) asserted:

> Its economic basis has shifted from the direct servicing of the black community to the state, with employment in public bureaucracies accounting for most of the growth of professional, managerial and technical positions held by African Americans over the past thirty years. The genealogical ties of the black bourgeoisie to the black poor have also grown more remote and less dense. (p. 104)

From this quote, we note the growing stratification in the Black community as the Black middle class separates themselves from the Black poor. Many scholars and authors have warned of the increasing separation, segregation, and stratification within the Black community (Dyson, 2005; Kitwana, 2002; Kunjufu, 2002; West, 2008). West (2008) elaborated,

"Once we lose any sense of a black upper or black middle class or a black upper working-class connecting with the black underclass with a 'we' consciousness or sense of community, it becomes much more difficult to focus on the plight of the poor" (p. 57). The evolution of the hyperghetto has become a place of increased violence, illicit drug sale and use, economic depravity, police surveillance and brutality, and struggling schools.

It is apparent that today's Black youth (the current generation) have been impacted by certain sociopolitical forces. Kitwana (2002) identified six major phenomena that make the lives of these youth different from those of previous generations: (1) a different process of values and identity development; (2) globalization; (3) persisting segregation; (4) public policy regarding the racialization of the criminal justice system; (5) overexposure and negative exposure with regard to media representation; (6) the decline in overall quality of life for the poor and working poor. In reference to values and identity formation, there is evidence that they are influenced in different ways. In the past, church, family, and school heavily influenced Black youth identity development (Kunjufu, 1993). Regarding today's identity development, Kitwana (2002) insightfully wrote:

> Today the influence of these traditional purveyors of Black culture has largely diminished in the face of powerful and pervasive technological advances and corporate growth. Now media and entertainment such as pop music, film, and fashion are among the major forces transmitting culture to this generation of Black Americans...For the most part, we have turned to ourselves, our peers, global images and products, and the new realities we face for guidance. (p. 7)

In terms of globalization, today's Black youth have come of age in a time where we have witnessed the upward mobility of a select number of elites and the expansion of the middle class (including Blacks) (Dyson, 2004). At the same time, we have witnessed jobs moving away from urban areas and the increasing distancing of the haves from the have-nots (Kitwana, 2002; West, 2004). Contemporary segregation is not evidenced by signs and customs as in the Jim Crow era. "We certainly live in a more inclusive society than existed in pre-civil rights America. However, continuing segregation and inequality have made it especially illusory for many young Blacks. The illusion of integration allows for some access, while countless roadblocks persist in critical areas where Blacks continue to be discriminated against in often subtle and sometimes not so subtle ways" (Kitwana, 2002, p. 13). White and Cones (1999) agree that contemporary prejudice exists mainly in the form of institutional racism. They explain:

> Institutional racism exists where whites restrict equal access to jobs and promotions, to business and housing loans, and the like. White bankers and mortgage companies can secretly collaborate to redline a neighborhood so that such loans are nearly impossible to obtain. White senior faculty members in predominately white universities (public and private) determine who gets promoted to tenured faculty positions...Good-old-boys' clubs in the corporate structure determine who will be mentored and guided through the promotional mine fields. (p. 136)

Black youth witness the continuing legacy of segregation and racism and its impact on their lives.

Related to the persistence of segregation/racism is the criminal justice system and how it is skewed against people of color (particularly Black males). This is not to say that if one commits a crime one does not deserve punishment, but the eyes of justice should be blindfolded, making people equal before the law. For instance, young Blacks have grown up with laws that give more jail time for crimes involving crack cocaine as opposed to crimes that involve powder cocaine (largely the drug of choice for more Whites). They have been impacted by the explosive growth in prison construction, zero tolerance policies, and instances of police harassment and constant surveillance (Kitwana, 2002). Dyson (2005) asserted, "The increase in black incarceration was driven by political considerations, not a boost in, for instance, drug consumption" (p. 88).

Kitwana (2002) eloquently captured the sentiments of many Black youth when he stated, "The collapse of trust in law enforcement and the vilification of Black youth through crime legislation certainly play a role in the view Black youth share about legislation, law enforcement, and criminal justice" (p. 18).

The images of young Blacks are frequently misrepresented by the mainstream media and today's entertainment titans. Still today, young

Blacks are overrepresented on the news as criminals and menaces to society (Kitwana, 2002; White & Cones, 1999). In addition, a wave of so-called reality-based television programs now depicts many young Blacks as combative, aggressive, ignorant, materialistic, and sexually obsessed (West, 2008). According to White and Cones (1999) "Not only do European Americans believe that theses caricatures represent the reality of Black male life, but Black male youths [and female youths] may aspire to live up to these images because they are popularized and romanticized" (p. 72).

Finally, today's Black youth recognize the significant issues around quality of life in America. The wealth gap between the rich and poor continues to grow (Dyson, 2005; Kitwana, 2002; West, 2008). West (2004) chides the more recent overemphasis on money-based values or obsession with wealth attainment. He asserted, "It also redefines the terms of what we should be striving for in life, glamorizing materialistic gain, narcissistic pleasure, and the pursuit of narrow individualistic preoccupations—especially for young people here and abroad" (p. 4). Kitwana (2002) discussed the impact of West's statement on the hip-hop generation when he stated, "For us, achieving wealth, by any means necessary, is more important than most anything else, hence our obsession with the materialistic and consumer trappings of financial success" (p. 6). Thus, Black youth realize the rampant wealth inequality in the U.S. and have in many cases made a conscious choice to pursue materialistic gain. West (2008) again warned, "The marketplace culture of consumption undermines community, undermines links to history and tradition, and undermines relationships" (p. 31). This quote is particularly powerful in relationship to the historical context provided here.

The phenomena presented here are provided to paint a picture of today's contemporary context, especially for Black youth. We recognize that the other time periods we examined earlier related to Blacks in general. We emphasize Black youth specifically here because of the great curiosity around their contemporary plight. Other things that inevitably impact these youth include: employment, relationships, technological growth, and political engagement (Dyson, 2004; Kitwana, 2002) to name a few. Obviously, the world around these youth would impact their outlook on education.

Educational Attitudes

In the 21st century, Blacks find themselves in a place of great promise and peril. Today, there seems to be almost limitless opportunities for students who are dedicated, determined, and disciplined. We have even witnessed what some thought was virtually impossible—the election of a Black president of the United States of America. His success is powerfully symbolic for all children of color, but the structures that one must navigate remain intact. Even as we acknowledge the great progress of Black faces in high places (West, 2008) the data tell a different story. According to McKinsey & Company (2009):

- Avoidable shortfalls in academic achievement impose heavy and often tragic consequences, via lower earnings, poorer health, and higher rates of incarceration.

- For many students (but by no means all), lagging achievement evidenced as early as fourth grade appears to be a powerful predictor of rates of high school and college graduation, as well as lifetime earnings. (p. 6)

Kunjufu (2002) indicates:

- Black students comprise 17 percent of the U.S. student population. Black teachers comprise 6 percent of U.S. teachers. Black males comprise 1 percent of U.S. teachers.

- There is no staff of color in 44 percent of schools.

- Of inner-city teachers, 40 percent transfer within 5 years.

- One of every three Black males is involved with a penal institution while only one of ten male high school graduates is enrolled in college.

- Only 3 percent of Black students are placed in gifted and talented programs.

- If a Black child is placed in special education, 80 percent of the time the child will be male.

- Thirty-three percent of Black households live below the poverty line.

- In light of *Brown vs. Topeka* in 1954, schools have become more segregated since 1971. (pp. vii–viii)

These data paint a bleak picture for far too many Black youth. The obvious question for many is how can we account for the lingering challenges that continue to impede the educational progress of African Americans? The framework provided here gives some insight. Specifically, regarding educational attitudes, the emphasis on education for liberation seemed to decline with the dismantling of segregated, all-Black schools and increasing integration; the conversion of overt racist practices to covert racist practices in schools; and the change in the attitudes of students regarding the value of education. As previously noted, segregated schools provided Black children at the time with academic preparation as well as preparation for life in a world that saw them as inept, inferior, and incapable. Schools reinforced their spirits as segregated society tried its best to tear them apart. This created a kind of resiliency in these students (Perry, 2003). When segregation ended and integration came, many dedicated Black teachers and administrators lost their jobs (McCray, Wright, & Beachum, 2007). In addition, as the doors of opportunity began to open, Black students opted for other majors besides education (Kunjufu, 2002). Therefore, the educators who provided quality education were lost along with the pipeline that would replace them. In their place, white educators largely took up the task of educating Black students, with mixed results.

Today, the teaching force (along with administrators) is predominately White (McCray et al., 2007). As a matter of fact, the teaching core in the U.S. is mostly White and female (Kunjufu, 2002; Mizialko, 2005). This in itself is not inherently problematic. The key issue here is teacher expectations. "There are consequences of a primarily white, female, middle class, monolingual teaching force. The consequences are felt by multicultural, urban learners" (Mizialko, 2005, p. 177). Hancock (2006) agreed: "The reality that White women are on the front lines of urban education is clearly evident. While we continue to recruit and retain minority teachers, it is critical that we also focus our attention on helping to educate White women teachers about the realities of teaching students who may hold a different sociopolitical, sociocultural, and socioeconomic perspective" (p. 97). Additionally, Kunjufu (2002) also made the point that Black teachers could have negative attitudes and low expectations toward students of color. The great problem here is that even though we exist in a society in which the visible manifestations of segregation and alienation are absent (i.e., *Whites only* signs, *Jim Crow* laws, etc.), many students still readily get the message by other covert means that their skin color is inferior. Tatum (1997) discussed the concept of cultural racism, defined as "the cultural images and messages that affirm the assumed superiority of Whites and the assumed inferiority of people of color" (p. 6). Similarly, Delpit (1995) described specific examples where teachers would seldom interact with students of color and called this "invisible racism." It is up to all teachers to strive for equity and excellence for all students.

Black students today are strongly impacted by the world in which they live. Today's youth live in a world of high-speed information sharing, texting, and tweeting as major means of communication—life lived online on the Internet—and are used to having many options. Unfortunately, the way we still structure schools is grounded in a 20th century philosophy. Many Black students, especially those from the inner city, seem to concentrate on immediate gratification as opposed to long-term gratification (as with a good education) (Kitwana, 2002; Kunjufu, 2002). In addition, many youth have witnessed relatives who have graduated high school or attended college and still face discrimination or unemployment (Dyson, 2005). "To be effective teaching African American students, you must convince them that there is a 'payoff' in education" (Kunjufu, 2002, p. 101). Educators must provide an accurate and convincing portrait of career choices and reinforce the importance of a good education. In addition, education must be viewed as not only a means for financial gain, but a tool for personal development and self-actualization.

Complexities and Contradictions

Today, Blacks seem to be both loved and hated by mainstream society. As it stands, when a Black reaches the pinnacle of their field (sports, acting, journalism, medicine, academics, business, politics, etc.), they are hailed as examples and showered with praise. But for the vast majority of Blacks who are struggling to make a way for themselves, they are many times met with resistance, bitterness, sarcasm, and/or resentment (Bogotch et al., 2008; Dyson, 2004; Perry, 2003; Tatum, 2007; West, 2008). This dichotomized view allows the dominant culture to accept a certain select segment of the Black population while at the same time justify the unfair treatment of the great majority who have not reached such lofty heights as their privileged peers. In this manner, the illusion of true equality in American society is allowed to flourish. This is a serious and ongoing contradiction. This kind of contradiction also affects other areas such as hip-hop culture.

Hip-hop culture has emerged in recent years and clearly dominates the lives of many youth. West (2008) exclaimed, "Hip-hop music is the most important popular musical development in the last thirty years" (p. 122). White and Cones (1999) stated, "Hip-hop is a catch-all term for a contemporary, urban-centered youth lifestyle associated with popular music, break dancing, certain dress and hair styles, graffiti, and street language" (p. 96). Hip-hop culture has gone from primarily rapping, break dancing, DJ-ing, and graffiti to including dialects, attitude, expression, mannerisms, and fashion (Au, 2005; Kitwana, 2002). Regarding youth, Kunjufu (1993) asserted, "The ages between 13–17 are when they [teenagers] are particularly vulnerable to outside influence and before their values and ideas are fully developed (Kunjufu, 1993, p. 81). Furthermore, Kitwana (2002) wrote, "Today, more and more Black youth are turning to rap music, music videos, designer clothing, popular Black films, and television programs for values and identity" (p. 9). It is apparent that hip-hop culture has the ability to affect the values of youth in general and Black youth in particular.

Hip-hop (or rap) music is yet another form of musical expression that signifies, symbolizes, and structures the Black experience. The music itself, although born out of postindustrial blight and inspired by those who considered themselves outcasts, has transformed over time (Dyson, 2007; West, 2004). Some may now argue that it has become a reflection of the materialism and corporate structures it railed against during its initial phases. West (2004) elaborated:

An unprecedented cultural breakthrough created by talented poor black youths in the hoods of the empire's chocolate cities, hip-hop has now transformed the entertainment industry and culture here and around the world. The fundamental irony of hip-hop is that it has become viewed as a nihilistic, macho, violent, and bling-bling phenomenon when in fact its originating impulse was a fierce disgust with the hypocrisies of adult culture—disgust with the selfishness, capitalist callousness, and xenophobia of the culture of adults, both within the hood and in the society at large. (p. 179)

West is referring to hip-hop's more humble beginnings when the music was a form of expression, a canvas for lyrical creativity, and mechanism for sharing the trials and triumphs of urban existence.

In sum, hip-hop may very well be both overestimated and underestimated. It is overestimated by critics and detractors for blaming the music for a host of social ills that existed long before hip-hop came into being (e.g., rampant materialism, deadly violence, drug proliferation, and malicious levels of misogyny). West (2008) levied a fair critique when he wrote, "Too often, hip-hop still lacks deep vision and analysis. It's just escapism, it's thin. It's too morally underdeveloped and spiritually immature. In the end, it has to be more of a turning-to in order to constructively contribute" (p. 127). At the same time, hip-hop is underestimated because of its awesome potential to make money, motivate people, and inspire young minds. It cannot be expected to solve all of the problems in the Black community, but at the same time it does have the potential to at least "do no harm." Dyson (2007) eloquently described hip-hop as follows, "Hip hop is fundamentally an art form that traffics in hyperbole, parody, kitsch, dramatic license, double entendres, signification, and other literary and artistic conventions to get its point across" (p. xvii). If the message in hip-hop is disturbing, then its creators are trying to tell us something about the contemporary Black experience.

Discussion

Our discussion here has covered a great majority of the Black experience. The authors acknowledge that this brief analysis cannot begin to address the comprehensive and complex nuances involved in this kind of sociohistorical critique. It is our hope to shed a modicum of light for additional insight. What follows is a summation of the information gathered from our rendering of the Wacquant (2000) framework.

Context Matters

In each phase observed we acknowledged historical context. In addition, Blacks are linked to the occurrences, happenings, and experiences of the past. Moreover, this is not simply a form of misguided nostalgia when we discuss Blacks and their history. There are pitfalls to extreme forms of this. Dyson (1997) warned, "Nostalgia is colored memory. It is romantic remembering. It recreates as much as it recalls" (p. 117). Our perspective here advocates the recognition of the comprehensive historical experience, even when the memories are painful (i.e., slavery and segregation). The lesson here is to *respect* the history, and also to *protect* the history, so the next generation will not *reject* the history. The acknowledgment of our tragic past is necessary, even as Blacks begin to experience what some would consider modest success. West (2008) stated,

> It's easy to think that somehow, because there's been relative progress for a significant number of black people, that there has been some kind of fundamental transformation. Therefore, we lose sight of the degree to which the history of New World Africans, in this hemisphere for 400 years, still affects us all. (p. 50)

Ultimately, our perspectives, attitudes, and views of reality cannot be totally separated from our context.

Education for Liberation

Black people have historically struggled for the right to learn, be educated, and be liberated. Education has been valued even at a time when it carried harsh penalties and was against the law (Perry, 2003). As we observe the current statistics regarding Black students in terms of dropout rates, achievement gaps, etc. we must question current practices. Earlier, we discussed several problems in the American educational system. Here are some promising ideas:

- All educators should engage in continuous self-improvement/self-development. This may include additional readings/reading groups, professional development workshops, and/or attending educational conferences. The goal is to create educational environments that value both equity and excellence (Beachum & Obiakor, 2005).

- Teachers should strive to increase the rigor of their lessons, make their lessons relevant, and continuously build relationships with their students.

- Educational leaders should provide resources to support measurable efforts to create time and space for teachers and administrators to reflect on their practice, engage in discussion/debate, and imagine as well as develop new and innovative school structures, programs, and activities.

- Parents should monitor and manage their child's educational progress. Attend parent-teacher conferences if possible; if not, schedule a specific time to talk to their child's teacher(s). Parents should provide their child with a quiet place to study as well as the proper materials (writing utensils, books, computer, globe, dictionary, calculator, etc.) (Kunjufu, 2002).

- Community members should "hold all leaders and elected officials responsible and demand that they change current policy" (Gordon, 2006, p. 34).

Improving the situation regarding Black education requires individual as well as collective action. In this chapter, we discussed what different constituencies can do individually. The collective urgency is captured in the following quote, "We must demand that local communities provide the resources to educate *all* children, that the state and federal governments provide sufficient resources. The mandate of educating all of America's children rests on all of us" (Gordon, 2006, p. 34).

The Continuity of Culture

From our readings of Black's experiences in the U.S., we identified many complexities and contradictions. As a theme we continuously looked at the role of music in each historical epoch. The role of music is multifaceted. It was a way to communicate and share information during slavery. In segregation, it expressed the pain in the blues and the promise in spirituals. During the American Civil Rights/Black Power era it enhanced the struggle for freedom. Even today, the music still has the potential to do all of the things of the past or reflect the reality of today (as so much of the music seems to do). Music is indeed a form of entertainment and artistic expression. At the same time, it has meant so much more to Blacks. In all of the historical periods, the music is trying to tell us something. Encoded in the music are strife, distress, and powerful emotion. The music also can also contain joy, peace, contentment, jubilation, and hope. This is the magic of music, to be able to take listeners on a journey to places they may have never imagined, or to give the listener an in-depth look into the soul of the person or persons making the music. This is the essence of the Black experience; the highs and lows, the good and the gloom, the realization of the American dream in the midst of the American nightmare.

Conclusion

In this chapter, we have taken a sociohistorical look at the experiences of Blacks in the United States. Wacquant (2000) provided a framework of "peculiar institutions" that informed our work: (1) Slavery (1619–1865); (2) Jim Crow/Segregation (1865–1965); (3) Ghetto (1915–1968); (4) Hyperghetto and Prison (1968–today). In each era, we delved deeper into historical context, educational attitudes, and complexities and contradictions. The core of our work may be best expressed by West (2008) when he wrote, "Black people have never had the luxury to believe in the innocence of America. Although we've experienced the worst of America, we still believe that the best of America can emerge" (p. 23).

Chapter Two

Dealing with Cultural Collision

What Pre-Service Educators Should Know

I think your ears have lied to you
And your eyes have implied to you
That Urban means undeserving and absent of purpose
So give me back!!
Give me back my identity!!
Give me the opportunity
To break free of influential essentials that my community seeks
And have been lead to believe
Either from Hip Hop vultures disguised as moguls
Or mass media outlets that televise and overemphasize
What is deemed a destructive culture
Broadcast and typecast misguided black youth
That lives below the reality of broken homes, economic oppression, and a
  multitude of Half-truths
And finding no salvation in my inner city school
Because educators aren't there to educate
But instead baby-sit and dictate
Further reinforcing and filtrating the messages that distort who I am
And who I could grow to be
So I ask why haven't you extended your hand
To enhance my ability, expand my ideals and possibilities

Versus leaving me to discover my identity through manipulated mediums
And an environment that welcomes my bemused condition
I mean more to this society
My articles of clothing, vernacular, or demographic
Do not define me.
Contrary to popular belief I am also aspiring, inspiring, and operating as a prodigy
   born out of art
So it is evident that I have the ability to play more than just this part
But I am also a product of my surrounding…and my underdeveloped mind often
   has no protection . . .
Then difficult to discover my identity and direction
This is a burden that I cannot overcome alone
Give me something additional to relate to before I become prone
To embracing what is put into the universe to be adopted as my own
Way of thinking, living, feeling…I am a king on my way to being dethroned
Understand me rather than abandon me and pierce me with labels
This is when you find distrust, despair, and anger
I need positive influence to rival the issuance of negative imagery so common in my
   world
I am young, black, impressionable, but imperiled
Look at me!!

—"LOOK AT ME," A POEM BY KRYSTAL ROBERTS (OF ATLANTA, GA)

This poem gives an acute voice to the legions of voiceless young people who are trapped in neglected neighborhoods, segregated schools, and cultures of chaos. Addressing this reality, Smith and Sapp (2005) stated,

> The goal of educational psychology is to effectively solve problems. In many urban schools, many educational problems remain unsolved. As it stands, we can clearly identify the epidemic of failures for ethnic minorities.…Urban practitioners must become problem-solvers and functional decision-makers. As problem-solvers, they must value ethnic, linguistic, and racial differences to effectively teach in urban schools. (p. 109)

The dispositions and beliefs of pre-service educational professionals are of extreme importance. The fate of urban school children largely rests in the hands of educators who may not share the same cultural backgrounds as their students or clients (Kunjufu, 2002; Landsman & Lewis, 2006). Therefore, it is critically important for these individuals to understand social context, appreciate differences, and champion change for a more multicultural organization (Cox, 1994; Cox, 2001; Irvine, 2003). Sometimes the problem is cultural, where the culture of educators clashes with that of their students, thereby creating a phenomenon called cultural collision (Beachum & McCray, 2004). By critically examining and understanding youth culture, teachers can gain educational insight (i.e., how to tailor teaching strategies and arrange classroom management policies) and make significant connections with their students, which could help reduce many of the problems Black youth face in schools.

African American youth identity is unique and multi-faceted. Like all youths, it can be affected by a multitude of factors including parents, peers, music, school, television, religious influences, and life experiences (Harro, 2000). But for inner-city youth in particular, self-identity is a combination of unique complexities. These youth may face several critical issues such as socioeconomic despair, pressure from gangs, a lack of faith in institutions, and society's concentration on materialism and individualism (Berman & Berreth, 1997). Of the numerous influences and factors that shape youth identity, two sometimes conflicting factors, Black youth popular culture (hip-hop culture and television) and school culture, are of particular importance.

In this chapter, we will concentrate on the development of secondary school-aged urban youth (i.e., those in grades 7–12). The popular culture of urban Black youth will be examined by means of hip-hop culture and the media. Both of these variables have the awesome potential to shape youth identity. The American phenomenon known as hip-hop can affect youth in both positive and negative ways (Kunjufu, 1993). In a like manner, television too can exert a powerful influence over youth. The media has the power to alter the habits, feelings, and minds of young people, especially Black youth (Kunjufu, 1990), as will be discussed. This chapter was written to assist in the understanding of psychological and cultural/social forces on urban youth, with special emphasis on Black youth culture. This information is critically important for emerging teachers who will work with these impressionable young people.

Notions of Contemporary America and Schools

If you work hard, can you really be "successful" in America? How much of your success is due to individual merit (your own efforts)? To what extent do structural barriers inhibit the life chances of certain groups in America? Are schools agents of change or do they perpetuate the inequalities found in American society? Though they may not seem so at first, these are complex questions, and of vital importance for educators and professionals who deal with diverse populations.

Why can't we readily identify oppression, inequity, and injustices? The answer might very well be that we are socialized into believing and acting out various roles as related to race, class, gender, ability, status, age, and social class (Harro, 2000). Tatum (1997) stated that this socialization process is similar to smog in the air; we all breathe it and are inevitably impacted. This "smog" is found in notions of meritocracy, individualism, and old-fashioned hard work. The cultural ethos of the United States is full of idealistic concepts such as the Protestant work ethic and the Horatio Alger myth (belief in the idea of going from rags to riches, as applied to everyone equally). Such ideas are ingrained into the psyches of nearly all Americans. Writing about pre-service educators, Villegas and Lucas (2002) asserted:

> They are insensitive to the fact that power is differentially distributed in society, with those who are affluent, white, and male having an advantage over those who are poor, of racial/ethnic minority groups, and female. They lack an understanding of institutional discrimination, including how routine practices in schools benefit young people from dominant groups while disadvantaging those from oppressed groups; and they have an unshakable faith that American society operates according to meritocratic principles and that existing inequalities in social outcomes are thereby justified. (p. 32)

Thus, pre-service educators must be willing to question deeply held beliefs and to challenge foundational assumptions. Of course, one might think, "I made it, why can't anyone else?" Villegas and Lucas responded, "Because the educational system has worked for them [pre-service teachers], they are not apt to question school practices, nor are they likely to doubt the criteria of merit applied in schools" (p. 31). The next factor in understanding how cultural collision operates is to realize how people are affected by the geographic isolation of many urban areas.

The Urban Context and Popular Culture

For the purpose of this discussion, it is important to understand the significance of the urban context. Many urban areas across the nation are plagued with all types of social and community problems, and schools in these areas face challenges such as inadequate funding and teacher apathy. Neglect from external powers fuels the fire for the marginalizing and criticism of these schools (Ayers, 1994). The urban context clearly creates an environment that affects urban schools and the youth within them. "The situation in far too many schools is one of despair, poverty, isolation, and distress" (Obiakor & Beachum, 2005b, p. 13). Noguera (2004) wrote, "In poor communities, the old, persistent problems of overcrowded classrooms, deteriorating facilities, and an insufficient supply of qualified teachers and administrators remain largely unaddressed" (p. 176). These are but some of the serious problems urban schools, and sometimes districts, encounter. Inevitably, the attitudes and behaviors of urban youth of color begin to reflect the structural inequities that have created their environments. Kozol (2006) traced the segregation, poverty, and inequity found in such schools in his book, *Shame of the Nation*. At the same time, these problems have resulted in the increasing pseudo-police state found in many urban areas and schools (Wacquant, 2001), as well as feelings of alienation (Rothstein, 1996; Yeo & Kanpol, 1999).

Black popular culture tends to originate from this urban context. According to Damen (1987), "Culture is learned and shared human patterns or models for living; day-to-day living patterns; those models and patterns pervade all aspects of human social interaction; and culture is mankind's primary adaptive mechanism" (p. 367). Black popular culture was born amidst "social, cultural, political, and economic segregation—initially as a vibrant expression of black political and cultural strivings" (Guy, 2004, p. 48).

Gause (2005) stated that "popular culture is the background noise of our very existence" (p. 336). When we consider the origin, expansion, and influence of "Urban America," we realize that its inhabitants are molded and shaped by history, experience, and social-context. The global phenomenon known as hip-hop culture can be viewed as an expression of Black popular culture with its roots found in the plight and promise of the urban context.

Hip-Hop Culture

Hip-hop culture has a great influence on American youth. Hip-hop culture is a broad term that encompasses rapping, dj-ing, danicng, langauge patters, slang, fashion, graffiti and artistic expression, and attitude (Dyson 2001; Kitwana, 2002;White & Cones, 1999). In reference to its wider appeal, Kitwana (2002) asserted that, "Rappers access to global media and their use of popular culture to articulate many aspects of this national identity renders rap music central to any discussion of the new Black youth culture" (p.11). This emphasis on media opens up rap artists to audio and visual media. McCall (1997) wrote:

> Dr. William Byrd, a black clinical psychologist, pointed out that for young, impressionable people the mere fact that explicit gangsta lyrics are aired on the radio lends credence to their messages as truth. 'When you bombard someone with those messages, it causes conflict, even with those young people who may have been taught other values. With these rap messages, not only are they being bombarded with radio, they also get video.' So it's what you hear and what you see. It confirms that these are acceptable values in a subculture. (p. 60)

Therefore, this "message bombardment" can be influential to impressionable youth. Kitwana (2002) agreed, "Today, more and more Black youth are turning to rap music, music videos, designer clothing, popular Black films, and television programs for values and identity" (p. 9).

Hip-hop culture has become an integral part of the lives of many urban youth. Through its influence, they develop various ideas about sex, relationships, success, and life (Kunjufu, 1993). These influences can have positive or negative effects on youth identity. Hip-hop culture is expressed through songs on the radio, glamorized by video, and reinforced by peers. The result is a particularly powerful form of infiltration and indoctrination. Again, this influence can be good or bad. Most of the controversy surrounding hip-hop culture has to do with its emphasis on male chauvinism, open gunplay, and illegal drug usage.

Much of the criticism revolves around a certain mode of hip-hop expression called gangsta rap. Gangsta rap usually refers to a style of rap that emphasizes drug selling, hyper-macho posturing, disrespect for authority, the use of violence to settle disputes and gain respect, and negative attitudes towards women (Guy, 2004; Kunjufu, 1993; White & Cones, 1999). In reference to this form of rap, Dyson (1997) wrote:

> The gangsta rap genre of hip-hop emerged in the late '80s on the West Coast as crack and gangs ruled the urban centers of Los Angeles, Long Beach, Compton, and Oakland. Since hip-hop has long turned to the black ghetto and the Latino barrio for lyrical inspiration, it was inevitable that a form of music that mimicked the violence on the streets would rise. (p. 113)

In recent years, the label gangsta rap has seemed to apply less to the contemporary forms of hip-hop displayed in popular culture. Today, much of the music incorporates strands of hip-hop along with other themes, making it into an eclectic combination of macho-posturing, misogyny, violence, and materialism. Thus, gangsta rap is less identified as a societal pariah of previous years, but is now a common part of "normalized" hip-hop culture. Hip-hop culture affects the values of Black youth through various media, television being the most significant.

Television Media

The American media are a source of news, entertainment, and information that include radio, newspapers, the Internet, and television, to name a few. For our purposes, the authors will concentrate on the media as represented by television. The media have the ability to spread truthful and positive knowledge or to misrepresent people, events, and data. Unfortunately, the latter is often the case. Moreover, television is responsible for imagery that negatively influences youth and can affect youth identity (Bush, 1999).

Television is an important part of life to many Americans. Black youth, in particular, watch seven to eight hours of television a day, as compared to four and a half hours for white youth (Browder, 1989). Bush (1999) noted that "negative images presented in all of the media conspire with many hours of television viewing to produce a negative effect on Black children's self-image" (p. 36). In reference to Black youth and television, Browder (1989) observed the following:

- Black children tend to use TV as a source of role models. They imitate other people's behavior, dress, appearance, and speech.

- TV provides examples of relationships with members of the opposite sex.

- TV is used as a primary source of learning and perfecting aggressive behavior.

- Black children closely identify with television characters— particularly the Black characters. (p. 47)

Given the amount of television watched by Black youth and its influence on their development, the images portrayed by the television media become extremely important.

Television many times promotes gender stereotypes and negative images of Blacks. A study conducted by Patricia D. Mamay and Richard L. Simpson (as cited in Bush, 1999) concluded that "women in commercials were typecast according to three stereotypical roles: mother, housekeeper, and sexual objects" (pp. 35–36). This research indicates that television has the ability to affect the way people view gender roles.

In addition to its role in shaping gender stereotypes, the television media also influence many youth towards violence. For instance, a 14-year-old Black male was sentenced to life in prison for the murder of a 6-year-old girl; he had been imitating pro wrestling moves he watched on television (Ripley, 2001). Today's Black youth are many times criticized and labeled as violent or rebellious (Dyson, 1997; Kitwana, 2002). Though violent acts are sometimes perpetrated, Wilson (1990) asserted, "Deeds of violence in our society are performed largely by those trying to establish their self-esteem, to defend their self-image, or to demonstrate that they too are significant" (p. 54). This is not to excuse individuals for violent behavior, but it does provide helpful insight into fundamental (or other) influences that impact behavior. Moreover, the television media promote a value system based on materialism and immediate gratification (Kunjufu, 1990). Enticed by these values, too many youths resort to violence. Thus, television exposure to negative imagery could possibly encourage an inner-adversarial conflict of self-identity.

Identity Theory and Black Youth

Black youth who are matriculating through middle and high school deal with a considerable amount of transition. The transitions are related to grade levels, geographic location of schools, maturation, and identity development (to name a few). Considering the latter, young adults share a certain amount of curiosity, exploration, and discovery with regard to the development of identity (Tatum, 1997). However, Black youth in particular begin to examine their own ethnic/racial identities even more that their White counterparts (Negy et al., 2003). Tatum (1997) posited that "Given the impact of dominant and subordinate status, it is not surprising that researchers have found that adolescents of color are more likely to be actively engaged in an exploration of their racial or ethnic identity than are White adolescents" (p. 53). It is in this state of heightened identity awareness that salient and unconscious messages and imagery can influence ideas and values. Black youth are also more sensitized to society's view of them with regard to race. "Our self-perceptions are shaped by the messages that we receive from those around us, and when young Black men and women enter adolescence, the racial content of those messages intensifies" (Tatum, 1997, p. 54). Hence, identity development for Black youth is complicated by notions of race/ethnicity more than for their White peers, making adolescence a time of complexity and vulnerability. This situation creates the need for direction and guidance from influential individuals and institutions, one of which is the school.

School Culture

The school itself can have a major impact on the development of students. During school, students are afforded opportunities for academic, emotional, and social growth. Students interact with teachers and administrators within the educational environment that is founded upon certain values. Academics, opportunities for growth, different types of interaction, and value systems all play a role in a school's culture; school culture also shapes student identity.

A school is commonly defined as a place of teaching and learning. The culture of an organization is the set of values and beliefs of the organization, and these values and beliefs are normally shared with the majority of people in the organization (Cunningham & Cordeiro, 2006; Fullan, 2004; Karpicke & Murphy, 1996). Thus, school culture is the shared value system of a given school. Specifically, school culture involves certain components. According to Pawlas (1997), "The key components of a strong effective school culture include shared values, humor, storytelling, empowerment, a communication system for spreading information, rituals and ceremonies, and collegiality" (p. 119). School culture is important to all who are involved with the school.

The school culture can affect student identity. Banks (2001) noted that

> the school culture communicates to students the school's attitudes toward a range of issues and problems, including how the school views them as human beings and its attitudes toward males, females, exceptional students, and students from various religious, cultural, racial, and ethnic groups. (p. 24)

When the school's culture is characterized by value disagreement, lack of communication, and little collegiality among teachers and students; many students see themselves as incapable, incompetent, and worthless. However, when an environment promotes a school-wide value system, good communication, collegiality, and the utilization of ceremonies, students' attitudes are much more positive. Karpicke and Murphy (1996) agreed that a healthy school culture has a great impact on the success of students.

Taking all of this into account, we find that those teachers who are interested in changing a culture must first try to understand the existing culture. To do this, teachers would have to begin by understanding the various cultures that come to the schoolhouse on a daily basis, before attempting to impose another culture.

Intersection of School Culture and Black Popular Culture

Certain negative values as dictated by hip-hop culture and media influence many times conflict with the values of the school. Kunjufu (1990) noted that gangs and negative media promote immediate gratification and materialism, while many parents and teachers promote long-term gratification and qualities such as moral integrity and honesty. Kunjufu (1993) also stated that there is a concern about some hip-hop artists' misogynistic and violent messages. In effect, students obtain certain values from this segment of hip-hop culture and television media and then bring those values to the school. As a result, there is a conflict of value systems, which sometimes results in discipline problems and a lack of communication between students and educators. In addition, peers can have a great influence on each other, even more so than the influence of adults (Kunjufu, 1990). Thus, negative or unhealthy values can become pervasive because of the influence of peer communication and pressure. Furthermore, Black youth spend much more time with peers listening to music and watching television than they do having meaningful conversations with teachers and parents (Bush, 1999; Kitwana, 2002; Kunjufu, 1994). The task for educators, therefore, is to familiarize themselves with youth culture/value systems and realize the subsequent effect on youth identity.

Hip-hop culture has undergone tremendous growth as an artistic form of expression and fashion, as well as a money-making venture. Many have advocated censorship in order to curtail the negative influence of rap music. However, censorship may not be an appropriate or realistic response; for it sends the message that artistic expression can be stifled by those who simply disagree. But what are we to make of the violent themes readily found in hip-hop culture? In response to the over-emphasis on violence in hip-hop, Dyson (2005) explained,

> Hip-hop has been nailed for casting glamour on thuggish behavior and for heartlessly painting violent portraits of urban life. It's all true, but still, the whole truth of hip-hop as art form and, because of generational lag, as agita-

tor of adults, must not be overlooked....At its best, hip-hop summons the rich-
est response in the younger generation to questions of identity and suffering.
(p. 115)

Dyson (1996) wrote, "While these young black males become whipping
boys for sexism and misogyny, the places in our culture where these
ancient traditions are nurtured and rationalized—including religious
and educational institutions and the nuclear family—remain immune to
forceful and just criticism" (p. 186). Therefore, a certain amount of
responsibility must be placed on parents, guardians, and school officials.
In effect, parents and educators should take a greater role in involving
themselves in the lives of these youth. One must remember that hip-hop
culture has a business aspect and the supply will meet the demand.
What would happen if the consumers demanded more positive images?

The media also have to be held accountable for their negative
imagery. If not, then youth identity remains imperiled. Chideya (1995)
wrote, "In the final analysis, it's up to the reader and viewers to keep the
media honest...pointing out times that the media has [sic] misrepresented the African-American community can only make the community
better. The media belongs [sic] to all of us. If we want it to work, we have
to work" (p. 11).

Implications for Educators

In summary, there are many factors that influence the identities of urban
Black youth. Hip-hop culture, television media, and school culture do
have a serious impact on this particular group. At the heart of this analysis is the creation of a healthy and positive value system. Consequently,
those students who develop a strong value system have less chance of
being affected by negative aspects of hip-hop culture and misrepresen-
tation in television media, and more of a chance to be influenced by the
"positivity" exemplified in a healthy school culture.

Educators have a critical role to play in students' academic and
social development. First, they must recognize the inherent inequities
within our society and how they impact people, especially those in
urban areas. Secondly, it is important they realize how cultural collision

plays out in our schools. By acknowledging the background experiences of urban students, which includes their cultural expressions, educators can gain insight into addressing student behavior, communication, and values. Lastly, Milner (2006) proposed some questions for educators to consider as they begin to self-examine, referring to such self-examination as *relational reflection*. The questions are as follows: "(1) Why do I believe what I believe? (2) How do my thoughts and beliefs influence my curriculum and teaching [managing and disciplining] of students of color? and (3) What do I need to change in order to better meet the needs of all my students?" (p. 84). Serious attention to these issues and questions can cultivate greater understanding, thereby helping educators be more effective.

Educators engage students in a mutual process of liberation for completeness: "Completeness for the oppressed begins with liberation. Until liberation is achieved, individuals are fragmented in search of clarity, understanding, and emancipation. This liberation is not outside of us or created or accomplished through some external force. Rather, it begins with a change in thinking" (p. 85). The essence of this "education for liberation" is a change in thinking for educators, causing them to realize their own power with students and their potential in society.

Due to the increasing amount of cultural and social diversity in our schools, educators must embrace some degree of cultural pluralism as they find the right balance that promotes a healthy school climate (Villegas & Lucas, 2002). There should be a willingness and effort among educators to structure the school culture to ensure that individuals of diverse backgrounds are well-positioned to achieve, regardless of their predispositions in life. A school culture structured in a pluralistic manner can foster self-efficacy and self-determination in students who, as a result, may bring conflicting values from their environment (Banks, 1995). Thus, Banks (2001) insisted "The culture and organization of the school must be examined by all members of the school staff…in order to create a school culture that empowers students from diverse racial and ethnic groups" (p. 22). This is extremely important because it helps to ensure that students are not being labeled incorrectly and are not subjugated because of inadequate cultural capital. Therefore, it is important for educators to help such students develop the kinds of value systems that encourage positive self-identities, and to give them the legitimate opportunity to become successful in school, as well as in life.

Note

This chapter is a reprint from:
Beachum, F. D., & McCray, C. R. (2008). Dealing with cultural collision: What pre-service educators should know. In G. Goodman (Ed.), *Educational psychology: An application of critical constructivism* (pp. 53–70). New York: Peter Lang Publishing.

Chapter Three

Leadership in the Eye of the Storm

Challenges at the Intersection of Urban Schools and Cultural Collusion

Instead of nostalgia, we need serious, rigorous analysis and critical appreciation of black youth. Instead of attacks on hip-hop culture, we need sharp, just, well-informed evaluations of its artistic statements and ethical imagination. Black nostalgia must be replaced by an even stronger force: the historic black determination to remain undefeated by pessimism from within black culture, and paranoia from beyond its borders. We must not be prisoners of our present circumstances, of current events. We must be prisoners of faith.

—MICHAEL ERIC DYSON

We are caught in an inescapable network of mutuality, tied in a single garment of destiny. Whatever affects one directly affects all indirectly.

—MARTIN LUTHER KING, JR.

The aforementioned quotations provide a promising contextual and theoretical perspective for urban school leadership. Notions of community, opportunity, and mutuality should characterize all American schools. The guiding American promises of life, liberty, and the pursuit of happiness could more easily be achieved if we would seriously consider the feasibility of Dr. King's "single garment of destiny." However, the practical reality for far too many urban schools is one that reflects the despair, dire socioeconomic situations, and complex cultural ethos of numerous neighborhoods and countless youth. Despite serious problems, there is of course much good in the neighborhoods and the youth. Thus Dyson (1997) makes a call for more rigorous analysis and critical appreciation, as there is more to the story than what we might see on television or hear in trite superficial conversation. This complicated context creates a daunting situation for educational leadership in urban schools.

This essay has three purposes. First, to provide insight into urban youth culture, specifically examining Black popular culture. Secondly, to propose a framework for the analysis of youth culture (i.e., cultural collusion). Finally, to present considerations and implications for educational leaders in an era of heightened educational accountability.

Katrina, America, and Schools: Defining the "Real" Hurricane

As these words find their way from our minds to the page, the imagery and irony of Hurricane Katrina is still fresh in the consciousness of many. In 2005, this enormous storm destroyed much of the Gulf Coast of the United States, and for a short time forced America to deal with the issues of poverty, racism, and geographic isolation of our fellow citizens. Although the response from governmental agencies was minimal (at first), the American people opened up their hearts—especially to many of the African American residents—like never before. This response resulted in feelings of both pride and anger. The pride came from the thought of knowing that our fellow citizens can rise to the ethical occasion and live out the espoused egalitarian and communitarian values this nation posits on a daily basis. At the same time, the disaster resulted in angry feelings due not only to slow response times, but also from the fact that many of the people who were displaced from their homes had been in a bad situation long before the first rain drop fell…and no one seemed to care. New Orleans could have been almost any other major urban area with a substantially large population of African Americans (or people of color). Though many turn a blind eye to it, the same conditions and vulnerability exist in other cities where segments of the community are segregated socially, economically, and politically.

So, as we reflect on Hurricane Katrina, we also wonder about American schools. There are far too many schools similarly submerged in dire situations everyday; however, they suffer in silence because of geographical and social isolation. Will it take a national emergency to bring their suffering to the forefront? What is the ethical responsibility of those who are benefiting because of this situation? Is there a problem with response time from policy makers and educators? What is the impact on vulnerable youth in these schools? Could No Child Left Behind (NCLB) be exacerbating the storm? What should school leaders do as the educational winds blow, waters rise, and the situation becomes more desperate?

The connection between NCLB and Hurricane Katrina is not as much direct as it is metaphoric. On a *macro level*, NCLB creates the context in which educators operate. Those individuals with resources and means of escape can avoid the brunt of the damage caused by its fury. However, those in the most vulnerable positions (especially urban areas) take the brunt of the storm without adequate means for escape. Educators in urban areas must utilize new paradigms and approaches to deal with their unique challenges. What we are positing here is a framework for educators to deal with these challenges on a *micro level*. Metaphorically, the hurricane can be applied to both contexts, one being a larger national debate and the other a school-based emphasis for local issues. We will concentrate largely on the latter by focusing on youth culture (including popular culture), which is an area largely ignored by NCLB and surprisingly neglected by scholars and practitioners.

Keeping It Real Versus Realistic: Popular Culture and Youth Culture

Popular culture is market-based rather than aesthetic based....it is the culture that is most "popular" in an economic sense; i.e., what TV programs receive the most viewers, radio the most listeners, recordings the most buyers, and movies the most ticket-buyers. Although the study of popular culture encompasses a wide variety of issues—from clothing to popular activities to material culture—it is rooted in entertainment. (Cusic, 2001, p. 1)

According to Cusic, popular culture has an economic incentive, which is driven by the masses for their entertainment. At the same time, there are those who are of the opinion that popular culture has a deeper meaning to all of us. Gause (2005b) wrote:

> Popular culture is the very sea of our existence. In today's society, particularly U.S. society, we are bombarded on a 24-hour basis with mediated imagery and sound that shape our values, belief systems, and moral structures. The social institutions of our society—including families, public schools, and the communities in which we live and work—are affected and *infected*, as are those institutions engrossed in their own "traditions"—the legal, religious, and political communities. (p. 335)

Gause has alerted us to the fact that popular culture, when combined with mass communication and technologically enhanced deployment (i.e., Internet, iPods, and cellular phones), has the ability to permeate all facets of society. Since our institutions are not immune to this influence, it makes no sense to ignore the inevitable or obvious. Unfortunately however, the impact on youth culture is little acknowledged by educational leaders. A large rift seems to exist between adults and youth who are also divided along lines of culture, experience, income, and social reality (Guy, 2004; Kitwana, 2002). For educational leaders in particular, it is important that they effectively assess and address the situation for the overall betterment of the students. Thus, understanding the ways in which popular culture affects and infects urban youth is critical to the success of educational leadership in urban areas. Similarly important is an understanding of the urban educational context dominated by the mandates of NCLB.

Who Really Gets Left Behind?
NCLB and Urban Schools

The reauthorized Elementary and Secondary Education Act (ESEA), also known as the No Child Left Behind (NCLB) Act, has led to increased

males aged 15–19 are murdered at a rate more than seven times that of White males in the same age group.

- Gunfire killed 3,365 children and teens in 1999—more than 38 % (1,301) were Black youths.

- The number of juveniles murdered peaked in 1993 at approximately 2,900 young lives. Although this figure has dropped by more than half to 1,300 juveniles murdered in 2000, a disturbing 45 % were Black youths. (Children's Defense Fund, 2003)

The idea of a culture of violence may help to explain some of the negative outcomes that play out in urban communities. Swift and extreme violence is utilized in several situations, such as settling disputes, vengeance, having one's hat turned in the wrong direction, being from the wrong part of town, and even for "dirty" looks (Kunjufu, 1995; Patton, 1998). White and Cones (1999) agreed, "Kids are killed for being in the wrong neighborhood, wearing the wrong colors, dating the wrong girl, or looking at someone the wrong way" (p. 221). The violence that we see may be an outward expression of deeper issues.

In the culture of violence, Black male youths are far too often targets of rage. Conditions (poverty, utilizing physical intimidation to solve problems, hopelessness, etc.) can significantly increase the chances of becoming a victim. A deeper analysis reveals that a sense of displaced hostile aggression could also be at work. Black youth, like many inner-city dwellers, may feel a sense of alienation and marginalization from an apathetic and uncaring greater society (Dyson, 1997). In addition, institutionalized (and sometimes overt) racism can add to the already stressful situation for youth. Unable to strike out at the "unseen hand" that controls institutions and supports those in the dominant culture in America (Vance, 2001), many Black youth, in turn, lash out at one another.

Patton (1998) conducted a two-year ethnography studying the lives of gang members. Although the group included "hard-core" gang members, he provided some interesting insight into the reality of many Black youths.

All the gang members in this study had stories to tell about the violence they had encountered at the schools they were supposed to attend. For them, school was not any safer than being out on the streets and many of them laughed when they described how school administrators dealt with gang violence. (p. 59)

Gang members by no means represent the perspectives and realities of all Black youth, but they do describe a culture in which other Black youth live. School officials seemed oblivious to the problem of violence in the school as these youth told stories about "control" of certain bathrooms in the school, with teachers even being afraid to enter. Sadly, too many Black youth in urban areas are navigating a violent minefield where one wrong step could mean a physical confrontation and even death.

This culture of violence has a long history in the United States, going back to the removal of Native Americans from their land to the kidnapping, torture, and forced labor of Africans for some 246 years (Kailin, 2002; Kunjufu, 2001). Violence is very much a part of mainstream America; it is viewed on our television shows, movies, and in our popular culture (Bush, 1999; Kunjufu, 1993). "It is simply dishonest to paint black youth as the primary source of violence in America…networks average 25 acts of violence an hour. By the time kids reach elementary school, they've seen 100,000 acts of simulated violence" (Dyson, 1997, pp. 141–142). Along with violence is a pervasive gun ethos in the United States. Dyson (1997) noted:

> In 1990, for instance, there were 11,730 people killed by handguns in the United States. In the UK, the figure was 22. In the US there are 201 million firearms in the hands of private citizens; 67 million of these are handguns. Every day, 65 Americans are killed by handgun fire. There are 1 million automatic or semi-automatic weapons circulating in our nation. (p. 143)

Although youth of color within urban areas are characterized as hyperviolent, clearly the legacy of violence engulfs the entire nation.

Materialism

Taking a cursory glance at urban youth culture, a pervasive culture of materialism is readily apparent. The culture of materialism relates to obsession with money, clothes, cars, and other flashy items. Akbar (1984) noted that the concentration on obtaining impractical items dilutes wealth and keeps Blacks focused on token power, rather than striving for authentic power fueled by economic responsibility. This ethos places a high value on tangible objects that give the outward appearance of wealth and/or power. These items can include anything from jewelry, expensive clothes, and cell phones, to cars and trucks fully equipped with sound systems, speakers, and televisions.

In order to understand this culture of materialism, one must understand its complex socio-historical context. A cursory glance could lull one into overemphasizing the individualistic intent of these youth. In the central-city environments that we are speaking of, there is a situation characterized by limitations. Therefore, some might equate the acquisition of material items as a symbol of success, much like the rest of the country does. Dyson (2005) opined, "Hip-hop culture has also been blamed for giddily embracing consumerism, a charge that is true, again, but even truer of whiter and richer segments of the culture...the perception of black youth consumption is often blown way out of proportion" (p. 115). He has highlighted the point that materialism is endemic in our culture, impacting people of all classes. "Moreover, the materialism that obviously can strike poor folk as well is, nevertheless, far less likely to do them or society as much harm as it does those with far greater wealth in this country" (Dyson, 2005, pp. 82–83).

Some would also state that the focus on materialism is the result of socioeconomic isolation from beyond the borders of inner cities. Wacquant (2001) asserted, "the task of defining, confining, and controlling African Americans in the United States has been successfully shouldered by four 'peculiar institutions': slavery, the Jim Crow system, the urban ghetto, and the novel organizational compound formed by the vestiges of the ghetto and the expanding carceral system" (p. 99). The idea of external control of a group (African Americans in this instance) is nothing new, especially with regard to American history. The movement, choices, and very lives of African Americans were regulated during antebellum slavery as well as during segregation (Blassingame, 1979; Perry, 2003). In a socio-historical sense, the choices of African Americans have always been shaped by this external control. The difference now is that we live in a post-Civil Rights America where the popular idea of individual choice tends to outweigh structural impediments to progress, which can be concrete or imponderable (Dyson, 2005). However, some would argue that in this era, those who inhabited the "Dark Ghetto" of the pre-Civil Rights world now are the residents of a hyper-ghetto, one that has suffered from the extra pressures of the exodus of jobs and professionals, the decline of manufacturing and industrialization, and the rise of a sense of hopelessness and helplessness (Wacquant, 2001; West, 1994). Thus, any discussion of the choices of inner-city inhabitants must be made with this in mind.

Misogyny

Misogyny can be defined as the hatred or distrust of women. It is also an unfortunate characteristic of hyper-macho urban youth culture. Contemporary youth culture is impacted by a persistent pseudo-pimp theme. In his characterization of life on college campuses, Kevin Powell (2003) asserted:

> For college is simply a place where men, irrespective of race or class, can—and do—act out the sexist attitudes entrenched since boyhood. Rape, infidelity, girlfriend beat-downs, and emotional abuse are common, and pimpdom reigns supreme. There is the athlete pimp, the frat boy pimp, the independent pimp, and the college professor pimp. (p. 58)

This attitude is spawned from the same cultural crucible that birthed violence and materialism (hooks, 2004). In fact, violence, materialism, and misogyny frequently operate together, feeding off one another (hence the term *cultural collusion*). The outcomes of this misogynistic mind frame include a false sense of gender-based superiority over women, the objectification of women as sex objects, and the active belief that gender is a determinant of mental/emotional capability and life trajectory.

Misogynistic and sexist attitudes and behaviors are part of the American landscape. Many such attitudes can be attributed to learned behaviors, but also television. Black youth in particular are susceptible to television's lure and influence as they spend large amounts of time watching it. "Negative images presented in all of the media conspire with many hours of television viewing to produce a negative effect on Black children's self-image" (Bush, 1999, p. 36).

Given the amount of television watched by Black youth, and its influence on their development, the images portrayed by the television media become extremely important. Television many times promotes gender stereotypes. The impact of a culture of misogyny is even more apparent when one combines the work of Katz (1995), who stated that "stressing gender differences in this context means defining masculinity in the opposition to femininity. This requires constantly reasserting what is masculine and what is feminine. One of the ways that is accomplished, in the image system, is to equate masculinity with violence (and femininity with passivity)" (p. 135). The culture of misogyny is also confirmed by Patton's research (1998); he observed that the culture of male gang members was one that was "patriarchal and women were not considered the equal of males" (p. 62). Although television influence and male gang culture do not reflect the totality and diversity of Black youth culture, both provide cultural cues and highlight very real circumstances and situations.

Ultimately, a culture of misogyny is harmful for everyone. For women, it subjects them to emotional and physical harm, lessens their quality of life, and forces them into myopic male-determined roles. For men, it engenders a false reality and undermines genuine mutually beneficial relationships (Powell, 2003). Katz (2000) contextualized the problems of a culture of misogyny when he opined:

> The level of male violence against women in this society is out of control. Despite decades of feminist activism, boys and men are still sexually abusing, battering, raping, and murdering girls and women at an alarming rate. While this violence has no single cause, the dehumanization and objectification of women in the media is surely one of the contributing factors. Consider the pervasiveness of sexual harassment that women suffer from men in school, the workplace, on the street. Men aren't biologically programmed to harass women. We learn it. (p. 250)

Therefore, urban youth (males in this case) learn sexism and promote the same cultural values they learn from others and institutions. In response to the criticism heaped upon such youth, Dyson (1996) retorted:

> While these young black males become whipping boys for sexism and misogyny, the places in our culture where these ancient traditions are nurtured and rationalized—including religious and educational institutions and the nuclear family—remain immune to forceful and just criticism (p. 186).

This problem is indeed pervasive, persistent, and powerful. It is not just about the hyper-macho posturing of Black males or urban youth, but the moral mirrors that we all must face with regard to how we see gender in American society.

Hip-Hop Culture

Hip-hop culture supports and promotes the aforementioned cultures operating within a Black youth culture. Hip-hop culture has grown from simply rapping, dancing, and dj-ing to include videos, language patterns, expression, mannerisms, and world views (Au, 2005; Kitwana, 2002). This particular culture is of importance because of its influence over youth. Hip-hop culture has the ability to sustain and maintain the cultures of materialism, violence, and misogyny through the transmission of messages or values (Gause, 2005a). In previous generations (e.g., 1920s, 1930s, and 1960s) there was a greater propensity for Black youth to draw values from community strongholds: families, religious institutions, and schools (Guy, 2004; Kitwana, 2002). In addition, Kitwana (2002) wrote, "Today, more and more Black youth are turning to rap music, music videos, designer clothing, popular Black films, and television programs for values and identity" (p. 9). It is apparent that hip-hop culture has the ability to affect the values of Black youth through various media.

Hip-hop culture is also unfairly stigmatized. It has been burdened with the ills of violence and devuant behavior, disrespectful attitudes, and the disrespect of of women (Guy, 2004; Kunjufu, 1993; White & Cones, 1999).

In response to this criticism, Dyson (2005) explained,

> Hip-hop has been nailed for casting glamour on thuggish behavior and for heartlessly painting violent portraits of urban life. It's all true, but still, the whole truth of hip-hop as art form and, because of generational lag, as agitator of adults, must not be overlooked...At its best, hip-hop summons the richest response in the younger generation to questions of identity and suffering. (p. 115

Leadership Matters: Implications for Educational Leaders

It was bad enough to witness the government's failure to respond to desperate cries of help scrawled on the tattered roofs of flooded homes. But Hurricane Katrina's violent winds and killing waters swept into the mainstream a stark realization: the poor had been abandoned by society and its institutions, and sometimes by their well-off brothers and sisters, long before the storm. We are immediately confronted with another unsavory truth: it is the exposure of these extremes, not their existence, that stumps our national sense of decency (Dyson, 2006, p. 3).

The aforementioned quotation by Dyson reinforces the notion that leadership matters. It also calls attention to the social responsibility we all must share in the human experience. Once again, using the Hurricane Katrina debacle as a metaphor for schools, where is the educational leader in all of this? Watkins (2004) asserted, "Public education is in the eye of the storm" (p. 2). We would add that educational leaders are also in the eye of the storm. And from the eye, they have unique vantage points. They enjoy relative though sometimes temporary safety; they also can see additional storms approaching. In their effort to optimize learning, liberty, and living, educational leaders should lead from the center of what appears to be educational chaos. It is our contention that a significant storm in many urban areas is the very issue of cultural collusion, and that educational leaders can deal with it by utilizing aspects of Robert J. Starratt's (1991) conception of critique, justice, and caring.

Critique

The ethics of critique, justice, and caring are interconnected. "None of these ethics by itself offer a fully adequate framework for ethical judgments; together however, each ethic complements the others in a developmental context of practice" (Starratt, 1991, p. 186). In dealing with cultural collusion, a multi-dimensional framework is most appropriate. This approach begins with *critique*. In order to fully understand how cultural collusion operates and flourishes, it is important to develop a critical consciousness. This consciousness encourages leaders to ask bigger questions about what they see occurring in their schools and in the world. Starratt (1991) expounded:

> Whether considering social relationships, social customs, laws, social institutions grounded in structural power relationships, or language itself, thinkers must ask questions such as the following: 'Who benefits from these arrangements?' 'Which group dominates this social arrangement?' 'Who defines the way things are structured here?' 'Who defines what is valued and disvalued in this situation?' (p. 189)

Ryan (2006) agreed:

> Being critical means becoming more skeptical about established truths. Being critical requires skills that allow one to discern the basis of claims, the assumptions underlying assertions, and the interests that motivate people to promote certain positions. Critical skills allow people to recognize unstated, implicit, and subtle points of view and the often invisible or taken-for-granted conditions that provide the basis for these stances. (p. 114)

Discerning educational leaders realize that cultural collusion is a product of a certain socio-historical context rooted in the urbanized and "racialized" experience in America. Thus, violence, materialism, misogyny, and hip-hop culture's influence is not viewed simply as the wayward misdeeds and moral failings of today's urban youth, but rather as a critical reflection of how the same influences impact the greater society. Dyson (1997) elaborated,

> There is a perception of aesthetic alienation and moral strangeness in black youth. Both of these perceptions, I believe, depend on a denial of crucial aspects of history and racial memory. Amnesia and anger have teamed up to rob many blacks [and others] of a balanced perspective of our kids. (p. 119)

The value of leaders who are critical is that they use their critical consciousness to provide history and context for a more balanced perspective of urban youth. English (2004) warned of the danger of existing in a "contextualess" vacuum. Leaders who value this form of critique are engaged in a liberated mindset, virtually free from the confusion of misinformation, stereotypes, and stigmatization.

Justice

Starratt (1991) noted that an ethic of justice was the second step in building an ethical school. Our usage of *justice* to address cultural collusion is similar. "Urban school leaders, especially building principals, have an incredible amount of discretion with regard to how justice is enacted in their schools. Their conceptions of justice must be tempered with a keen understanding of the socio-economic plight of their communities" (Beachum & Obiakor, 2005, p. 94). Basically, the keen insight of the communities and the experiences gathered from critique are incorporated into a more practical form of decision-making. A major issue with justice is governance. Educational leaders must balance their responsibilities to the greater school community—its norms, rules, and regulations—for the purpose of creating a safe and orderly educational environment. At the same time, they must protect student rights and create an environment that fosters individual growth, freedom of creativity and uniqueness, and freedom of expression (Starratt, 1991). These efforts constitute a significant organizational paradox for almost any educational leader in various contexts. For leaders in urban contexts in which cultural collusion operates, the problem is exacerbated. Thus, educational leaders must know when to censor student movement, speech, or practices, especially when manifested in negative behaviors (i.e., fights, sexually harassing other students, etc.), which may be outcomes of cultural collusion. Similarly, hip-hop culture is sometimes at odds with the school culture (Au, 2005; Beachum & McCray, 2004). According to Tatum (1997),

> Certain styles of speech, dress, and music, for example, may be embraced as 'authentically Black' and become highly valued, while attitudes and behaviors associated with Whites are viewed with disdain. The peer group's evaluation of what is Black and what is not can have a powerful impact on adolescent behavior. (p. 61)

Many times what is "authentically Black" is intimately connected to hip-hop culture (Au, 2005; Kitwana, 2002). Ginwright (2004) agreed, "To seriously discuss black youth identity, educators, policy makers, and researchers must consider the inseparable relationship between black youth identity and hip-hop culture" (p. 32). The approach spoken of here seeks not to mute student expression or stifle hip-hop culture, but to encourage counter-cultural realities to refute the mixed messages urban youth might receive in a context of cultural collusion. This justice orientation is complimented by an ethic of caring.

Caring

Starratt (1991) completed his ethical framework with the ethic of caring. Caring is both a process and a product. Starratt (1991) concluded that "caring recognizes that it is in the relationship that the specifically human is grounded; isolated individuals functioning only for themselves are but half persons. One becomes whole when one is in relationship with another and with many others" (p. 195). "Care means liberating others from their state of need and actively promoting their welfare; care additionally means being orientated toward ethics grounded in empathy rather than dispassionate ethical principles" (Walker & Snarey, 2004, p. 4). Caring involves compassion (Gilligan, 1982), sincere dialogue (Freire, 1973), and modeling (Cunningham & Cordeiro, 2003). Compassion is the capacity for sharing the interests of another. It is a key component in caring. Educators who show compassion tend to make genuine connections with students (Kunjufu, 2002). For urban youth engulfed in cultural collusion, compassionate leadership can be critical. Another component of caring is sincere dialogue. Leaders should foster serious and sincere conversations around issues of race/ethnicity, gender roles, class, and oppression (Dantley, 2005; Gause, 2005b). Through this engaged process, teachers and administrators can begin to counter the many negative messages youth receive as a result of cultural collusion. Modeling is a crucial aspect of caring. From modeling, youth see caring in action, which makes it easier to imitate. Furthermore, modeling caring builds credibility, especially for many urban youth who can easily detect whether or not an adult is authentic (Kunjufu, 2002). Noddings (1992) opined, "Modeling for educators means demonstrating to students that we care, rather than just saying it" (p. 17). Fullan (2001) pointed out that modeling has the ability to "improve the performance of the organization while simultaneously developing new leadership all the time" (p. 132). This is an important factor for students, that is, to see the leadership in schools actively and actually living the values they espouse; and it helps deter skepticism and accusations of hypocrisy.

Conclusion

> Today, more than fifty years after the Brown decision, culturally and racially different children still attend schools that are generally segregated and underfunded. Although some progress has been made in closing achievement and graduation gaps, there is still much room for progress. We have entered the 21st century in a political climate that does not promise strong national support for increasing funding for urban schools…NCLB is long on rhetoric and mandates but short on financial resources. (Epps, 2005, p. 231)

This quotation captures the contemporary plight of urban schools. It illuminates a harsh financial and social reality that reflects the neglect of and distain for many urban communities. For the schools in these communities, educational leaders must find effective means of dealing with difficult realities. The advice of many researchers is too esoteric, too theoretical, or non-actionable (Fullan, 2004; Tillman, 2006). What we have presented here in the concept of cultural collusion is a way to frame what many educators see and experience on a daily basis. The emphasis on youth culture is critical because

> The divide between the hip-hop generation and that of our [their] parents has not yet registered on the radar screen of cultural critics, activists, or policy makers. It is a divide that is as vast as the one that separated white America in the 1960s, as radical white youth culture broke from the mainstream and swept across the country. (Kitwana, 2002, p. 22)

Dr. Martin Luther King, Jr. once stated, "An individual has not started living until he can rise above the narrow confines of his individualistic concerns to the broader concerns of all humanity" (King, 1987, p. 3). The challenge for school leaders is to "walk the talk" and to encourage this kind of uplift in their school community. Cultural collusion provides a framework for people to better understand how culturally-related factors such as violence, materialism, misogyny, and hip-hop merge, mesh, and shape the realities of urban youth and especially youth of color. Cultural collusion presses on like a hurricane in many urban schools, and leadership in the eye of the storm requires rigorous critique, an authentic commitment to justice, and heartfelt caring. At the same time, we must acknowledge the fact that the storms of cultural collusion are not confined to the shores of urban communities, but rather, they strike with vicious winds of influence and rains of realities, which soak into the psyches of all Americans. Dyson (1996) agreed, "Corporate capitalism, mindless materialism, and pop culture have surely helped unravel the moral fabric of our society" (p. 186). Educators in general and educational leaders in particular must realize the power, effect, and impact of popular culture. Ultimately, educational leaders should heed the words of Gause (2005b) when he stated, "Popular culture is a dominating force in our society. We must acknowledge its effects and usages in the educational process" (p. 341).

Note

This chapter is a reprint from:
Beachum, F. D., & McCray, C. R. (2008). Leadership in the eye of the storm: Challenges at the intersection of urban schools, cultural collusion, and *No Child Left Behind*. *Multicultural Learning and Teaching*, 3(2). Available: http://www.mltonline.org/current-articles/mlt-3–2/beachum-mccray.pdf

Chapter Four

The Ramifications of Cultural Collision and Collusion

How Young Black Males Are Being Ushered Out of Education

In America in 1900, the mean level of schooling completed was seven years, and a quarter of the population had finished four years or less. The mean today is two years of education after high school, or fourteen years, and the great majority of people complete high schools

(RICHARD E. NISBETT, 2009, P. 43).

Adolescent Black males today are in a precarious state of affairs as they attempt to navigate through school as well as life itself (Wilson, 2009). The statistics concerning young Black males are alarming. The American Civil Rights Movement along with *Brown v. Board of Education* and the plethora of legislation passed in the 1950s and 1960s have not had the intended consequences that were hoped for concerning young Black males, especially Black males from the inner city (Collins, 2005). Collins (2005) opined that "for Black youth who feel they have 'nothin'(sp) to lose because they lack access to the housing, education, health care, and jobs needed for upward social mobility, the political victories of the civil rights and Black power movements failed to produce the promised economic development envisioned by civil rights activists" (p. 78). Alas, anecdote after anecdote concerning Black males in inner city schools from impoverished backgrounds provides a narrative that is increasingly creating a chasm between not only Anglo-Americans but between middle-class Blacks as well (McCray, 2008). Thus, it is not entirely inconceivable that today's young Black boys are standing alone on an island engulfed by the rudiments of once booming heterogeneous neighborhoods that have now become simply the *hood* (Shelby, 2005).

The prescription needed to reverse the course of this alarming state of affairs young Black males have found themselves in is complicated; however, as this chapter will demonstrate, the most prudent undertaking that should be advocated for is to reduce the number of Black males who are dropping out of school. As noted in the opening quote by Professor Nisbett of the University of Michigan, most Americans today complete their compulsory education and go on to at least two years of post-secondary education. But, unfortunately, the statistics are not as incandescent for many Black males in urban areas (Gregory & Mosely, 2004; Thomas & Stevenson, 2009). It is not surprising that students who are unable to complete their compulsory education are more prone to a life of uncertainty and are more likely to go through the penal system (Day-Vines & Day-Hairston, 2005; Wilson, 2009). They also are more likely to be unemployed as well as underemployed (Alexander & Entwisle, 2001). According to Day-Vines and Day-Hairston (2005), "52% of African American males who departed prematurely from school had prison records by their 30s. Current projections indicate that 32% of African American males are likely to serve prison terms" (p. 237). Long before young Black males from the inner city decide to drop out of school and render themselves to the harsh environment that results from not completing a compulsory education, the conditions leading to failure have been cultivated by the students themselves, as well as the school officials and educators whose job it is to assist the students in the educational process. Research has shown that students who are subject to expulsion and suspension are less likely to complete high school (Peterson, 2003; Skiba & Peterson, 1999). In fact, according to Skiba and Peterson (1999), "Over 30% of sophomores who dropped out of school had been suspended, a rate three times that of peers who stayed in school" (p. 28). Thus, based on such statistics, it is incumbent upon school officials and educators to recognize and adequately address the *cultural collision and collusion* that is ushering young Black males out of their educational opportunities.

The Operationalization of Cultural Collision

The aforementioned collusion that is negatively affecting young Black males occurs when educators and administrators engage in symbolic educational trenched warfare to create *undesirable conditions* for the *undesirables* (Peterson, 2003). The *undesirables* are those who are experiencing a cultural collision (Beachum & McCray, 2004; Beachum & McCray, 2008; Day-Vines & Day-Hairston, 2005) within the established mores of the school. This cultural collision is where students bring their own culture into the school, a culture that is many times undergirded by the *code of the streets* (Anderson, 1999; Wilson, 2009). According to Anderson (1999), the *code of the streets* is a set of conventions embraced by young Black boys from the inner city that implicitly and explicitly direct their behaviors and dispositions toward others. Wilson (2009) indicated that the *code of the streets* is usually embedded with the notion of obtaining respect where far too often there has been none. Thus, educators and school officials seem to be ill-equipped to deal with the cultural collision that is taking place within their schools, and the corollary of cultural collision is the collusion that educators and school officials choose to engage in at the expense of young Black boys.

Just as hip-hop artist Rob Bass articulated in the 1980s that "it takes two to make a thing go right," the collusion among young Black males and educators seems to indicate that *it takes at least two to make a thing go wrong*. Thus, the definition of *cultural collusion* here is being expanded from what Beachum and McCray (2008) indicated in their previous works that defined *cultural collusion* as the co-opting of hip-hop by the three broader ills of our society: materialism, misogyny, and violence. Beachum and McCray (2004) and Beachum and McCray (2008) talked about how some hip-hop artists have fed into the general belief of the practices of materialism, misogyny, and violence. Beachum and McCray (2008) also conveyed how educators and society are quick to blame hip-hop and Rhythm and Blues (R&B) for such practices while turning a blind eye or being indifferent to the practices of materialism, misogyny, and violence by the broader society. Thus, this chapter will expand on the concept of *cultural collusion*. This expansion of *cultural collusion* is being undergirded by Ferguson's (2001) concept of *adultification*, a process that consists of educators and educational leaders assigning adult consequences on students when their behavior and mannerisms are not aligned with the school's culture. In order for the number of young Black males who are being ushered out of the schooling process to diminish significantly, educators and school leaders must be cognizant of how they are reacting to and treating young Black males from the inner city who come to school with little social and cultural capital.

Why Focus Exclusively on Black Males?

It is quite evident that many students from the inner city are experiencing turmoil within the educational system. Thus, in the spirit of Starratt's *ethic of critique*, why choose to focus exclusively on Black males when research has been adamant that there is no explicit disadvantage in American education toward boys (Corbett, Hill, & St. Rose, 2008; Thomas & Stevenson, 2009)? This research was made available by the American Association of University Women. Nevertheless, a specific focus on Black males is justified when the intersection of race, gender, and class is taken into account (Gregory & Mosely, 2004; Thomas & Stevenson, 2009).

In many instances, young Black males are not represented in Harro's (2000) *agent group* (i.e., privileged, upper class) category, but instead are represented in what Harro has identified as *target groups*. Target groups are the students of color, female students, students with different sexual orientations, students with different religious beliefs, and students from lower socioeconomic levels (Harro, 2000). They are often subjugated and disenfranchised (McCray, Alston, & Beachum, 2006). The corollary of target groups is the aforementioned agent group. According to Harro (2000), agent groups "have access to options and opportunities, often without even realizing it. Agent groups include men, white people, middle- and upper-class people, abled people, middle-aged people, heterosexuals and gentiles" (p. 17). So, by virtue of Black males being male, why are they represented in target groups? Part of the answer is that the intersection of race, class, and gender makes it a tumultuous challenge for young Black males to overcome the stereotypes and negative perceptions that this country has of Black men (McCray, 2008), especially Black men from the inner city. These stereotypes consist of the notion that Black males are oversexed and dangerous and are placed on this earth for their athletic prowess. Such stereotypes are operationalized in our schools emphatically by virtue of the achievement gap as well as the discipline gap (e.g., Black males more often are labeled as mentally retarded or placed in low-track classes, are punished in the classroom more often, and have higher suspension, expulsion, and dropout rates [Cassidy & Stevenson, 2005; Gregory & Mosely, 2004; McCray & Beachum, 2006; Stevenson, 1997; Thomas & Stevenson, 2009]).

In today's tough economic times, Black males also have the highest unemployment rate of any other group in the country (Cosby & Poussaint, 2007; Wilson, 2009). In addition, they are the only males of a particular ethnic group with a higher unemployment rate than their female counterparts (Wilson, 2009). In many of our urban schools, the dropout rate among Black males is approaching 50 percent (Cosby & Poussaint, 2007). Thus, the high dropout rate is exacerbating Black males' unemployment rate. Black males also are twice as likely to be unemployed than their White and Asian counterparts, and, unfortunately, such a high unemployment rate is having severe consequences on Black males revolving through the criminal justice system (Cosby & Poussaint, 2007; Wilson, 2009).

The connection between young Black males dropping out of school and their involvement in the criminal justice system is undeniable. Statistics show that an individual's prospect of making a decent living often is contingent upon an adequate education; the more advanced an individual's education is, the more likely an individual is to accumulate more wealth (Strayhorn, 2008; Wilson, 2009). Typically, the more advanced the degree that is obtained, the greater the chance for a better quality of life in terms purchasing power and lifestyle (Wilson, 2009). The baseline for an adequate education is the compulsory education that is mandated by the states. In most states, it is mandatory for students to attend high school up until a certain age. In many instances, this age is set at approximately 16 years of age. Unfortunately, many Black males in the inner city are not being afforded the opportunity to meet the baseline requirements for the lifestyle that many of them feel entitled to as young adults. Thus, the end result—due to the high dropout rates and the low chance for skilled employment—is that one in four of young Black males are matriculated in the criminal justice system instead of the higher education system. In addition, an alarming 60 percent of young Black males who have dropped out of school have spent time in prison (Cosby & Poussaint, 2007; Wilson, 2009). The corollary of such statistics is that young Black males engage in what Venkatesh (2006) coined the *code of shady dealings*, where many young Black males engage in an underground economy in order to supplement their lack of education and skill sets needed for today's *service and information economy*.

A Critical Self-Examination among Educators

It is critical for stakeholders such as parents, educators, and school leaders to become aware of the seriousness of the situation and begin to take on a serious self-examination and to interrogate and unearth the plethora of reasons why young Black males are being ushered out of the educational process. This self-examination among a multitude of parties is what is needed for such cultural collision and collusion to dissipate in earnest. School officials (i.e., teachers, administrators, and staff) cannot afford to pretend as if they are in no way culpable when it comes to this dire predicament that many inner city Black males find themselves in. As professors of educational leadership, we have heard far too many stories from our students indicating that the "parents and students just do not care about learning." We have also heard statements from our educational administration students such as, "They care more about Air Jordan's and 50 Cent CDs [the famous rapper from New York] than they care about school supplies"; "If 'these' students would put forth half the effort in their work like they place in memorizing the lyrics of Notorious B.I.G. [the New York rapper who was fatally shot and killed in 1997], they would be successful in their academic endeavors"; "It seems as if young Black males just do not have any pride about themselves...they constantly walk around with their pants sagging down to their butts....I don't want to see any of that"; "They use some of the worst language I have heard to date." It is unfortunate, but there is indeed a cultural collision that takes place on a daily basis between young Black males and their teachers, the majority of whom come from a different cultural background (Haberman, 2005). Thus, this chapter stresses the need for educators and school leaders to become more aware of how such a cultural collision and collusion is having a devastating impact on an entire generation of students. Educators and school leaders have less control over the self-examination that occurs among students and parents with regard to the culture collision that occurs within their schools. However, the cultural collusion that takes place when educators implicitly usher out students who do not bring the proper social and cultural capital to school is an area in which educators can make critical adjustments. In addition, educators and school officials must also recognize that young Black males from the inner city are not entirely homogenous with regard to their thinking, behavior, and dispositions toward school.

Little Room for Error

Ferguson (2001) found that young Black male students can either be identified as *schoolboys* or *troublemakers*. Ferguson went on to describe *schoolboys* as those students who were cognizant of their work and followed the edicts that the school had in place in order to be successful. Ferguson also found in her research that *schoolboys* usually came from families with a certain awareness of the cultural and social capital needed to succeed in school. Ferguson (2001) opined that there were instances where young Black male students came from such families but crossed over into the *troublemakers'* group. In fact, Ferguson found that Black male students are constantly resisting the temptation to be labeled as *troublemakers*. Ferguson proffered that the *troublemakers* were usually from families who were not readily cognizant of the cultural and social capital needed to be successful in academic endeavors. Thus, children from families who do not have a firm grasp on the school mores and values are at a higher risk of failing academically (Ferguson, 2001). Both *troublemakers* and *schoolboys* are subject to experiencing a cultural collision in their schools; however, *cultural collision* among the *troublemakers* increases exponentially.

This firm grasp of the school's mores and values is undergirded by the *schoolboys* being taught by their families the appropriate body language to display when interacting with adults. Ferguson (2001) found that Black male students often will display subtle body language gestures to indicate to adults their displeasure at what they perceive to be mistreatment and uncaring actions. Black families that have a sound understanding of the cultural and social capital needed to succeed in school also teach their children how to talk to adults in a respectful manner as well as how to dress in an appropriate way. More often than not, educators tend to give the benefit of the doubt to students who come to school appropriately dressed (i.e., having pants pulled up to their waist). And then there is always the issue of students following orders. Ferguson (2001) as well as Beachum, Dentith, McCray, and Boyle (2008) found that students who are most likely to get into trouble at school are those who are least likely to follow orders from their teachers and school administrators. In many cases, such orders are simple and not of dire consequences; yet if not followed precisely, especially by someone with little to no social or cultural capital, the ramifications can be severe (Beachum & McCray, 2008). For instance, if a teacher directs a child to come up to the teacher's desk at once, and if the student displays a slightly negative disposition and takes too much time getting to the teacher's desk, such an occurrence could lead to the student being sent to the principal's office. And depending on the student's past behavior, it could also lead to the student being sent to detention or, in some cases, being suspended (Beachum & McCray, 2008; Ferguson, 2001).

Black families who are aware of the *little room for error* axiom that young Black males face in their communities as well as in their schools teach their children how to control their dispositions and how to follow school rules as much as possible. The truism *little room for error* is observed among young Black boys and men on a daily basis (Ferguson, 2001). Whether they are trying to catch a cab, are being profiled by the police for driving a nice car in a nice neighborhood, or are being questioned and interrogated as to being in the right place (Shelby, 2005; West, 1994), young Black boys and Black men who are firmly aware of the cultural and social capital that is needed to succeed in life take very seriously the saying *"little room for error."* This axiom became operationalized for the national public once more when CNN, in April 2009, aired a report on racial profiling. CNN reported that in certain communities the police admitted to stopping young Black males on purpose, regardless of whether they were suspected of committing a crime. The purpose of this tactic was to instill fear in them and to make them afraid of the police. The rationale for such behavior is that crime among the Black males in certain communities is so bad that these are the tactics that must be deployed in order to fight *lawlessness*. Obviously, there is something severely wrong with the stopping of innocent individuals who have not committed a crime or caused any infraction for the sole purpose to striking fear into them. Hopefully, the Department of Justice will look into such tactics. Such situations are not unlike what is taking place in many urban schools across the nation. Unfortunately, in many of our inner city schools, schooling has ceased being an educative experience for many young Black males and instead has become a battleground over cultural values.

As noted earlier, it is quite evident that there is a link between success in life and acquiring at the very minimum a high school education. It is also quite evident that there are certain procedural and structural requirements that a person must be familiar with in order to ascertain this minimum requirement for success in the 21st century. However, caution should be exhibited when using such language as "quite evident" with regard to the requirements for success and achievement. For many individuals from inner city communities, it is not always transparent with regard to how to navigate the structural and procedural terrain in order to find success (Wilson, 2009). While young individuals from the inner city might have the best intentions of wanting to follow the rules and be successful in life, they often are misguided in their attempts and endeavors to get there. Such misguided attempts are exacerbated by the daily *collusion* that goes on in the school system. This collusion seemingly calls for the profiling of young Black males, whether they are *troublemakers* or *schoolboys*. It makes the axiom *little room for error* a truism, and it nullifies the notion of *good bad boys*, as far as Black males are concerned, and makes the prerequisite for success in school an unequivocal subscription to *good good boy* behavior (Ferguson, 2001). According to Fiedler (1960), the *good good boys* are the young men in our society who seem to do everything right. They are the young men who rarely find themselves in the slightest trouble at school or in their communities. And the corollary of the *good good boy* is the *good bad boy*. Fiedler (1960) operationalized this group as the young men who display a mischievous disposition. They break the rules ever so often by horseplaying, on occasion talking back, bending the rules slightly to their advantage, and playing naïve to the established edicts and rules. However, this conduct by the *good bad boy* is usually looked upon as *boys will be boys* when it comes to males with a *decent amount of social and cultural capital* (i.e., young boys who come from middle-class backgrounds) (Ferguson, 2001).

Even though most young adolescent boys with a sufficient amount of social and cultural capital have this space of negotiation and are well within their rights to navigate back and forth between the *good good boy* and the *good bad boy* personifications, this is a benefit that few Black male students can afford to engage in with regard to their academic careers as well as within their communities. In communities where police engage in hyper-racial profiling and look for any excuse to stop and interrogate a young Black male on a moment's notice, it is not difficult to imagine the outcome if young Black boys subscribed to the *good bad boy* persona. The fact that young Black boys are not able to safely engage in the *good bad boy* persona is because they have in essence been *adultified* by educators and law enforcement authorities (Ferguson, 2001). According to Ferguson (2001), "They are not seen as childlike but *adultified*; as Black males, they are denied the masculine dispensation constituting white males as being 'naturally naughty' [*good bad boys*] and are discerned as willfully bad" (p. 80). Thus, when young Black males make a *play* at females, they are looked at as oversexed; when they show the slightest sign of discontent through body language, they are seen as defiant, disobedient, hostile, and aggressive; and when they bend the rules slightly to their advantage, they are disparaged as *being up to no good* and *possibly cheaters* (Ferguson, 2001).

Ferguson's Adultification and Cultural Collusion

Ferguson's (2001) *adultification* process of young Black males in the inner city intersects with *cultural collusion*. This intersection has the propensity to impede the success of many of the brightest and most talented young Black boys. A notion that personifies this sentiment and is prevalent in the Black community is the aphorism that *some of the brightest and smartest young men [Black men] our locked up in prison*. As previously noted, there is a need for grave concern over the number of young Black men who are either in prison or have been through the criminal justice system. However, if there is any truism to the axiom that some of the brightest and most talented Black men are locked up in prison, it is certainly worthwhile to interrogate, unearth, and critique why there are so many bright, young Black men finding themselves part of the criminal justice system. Such a critique could take us in a multitude of directions. A surface-level critique and unearthing presents the obvious: Many young Black men find themselves in the criminal justice system because *they simply did the crime (in most cases, certainly not all) and had to do the time.* Another translucent conclusion is that it is no secret or surprise that the criminal justice system has historically been inherently biased when it comes to young Black men (Dyson, 2004). It seems that with the election of President Obama as the leader of the free world, it is almost passé to believe that there are still major issues with regard to race in the U.S. In reality, the historical mistreatment and the lingering effects of such mistreatment of Black males in the criminal justice system is well documented (Dyson, 1997; Dyson, 2004; White & Cones, 1999; Wilson, 2009). The critique of the issues young Black males face in our society must go beyond such axioms as *committing the crime and doing the time* and *the system is simply biased and racist*. Before the criminal justice system becomes intertwined with a young Black male's life from the inner city, it is imperative for educators and school officials to figure out a way to keep him in school by reducing the suspension and expulsion rates. Thus, how can educational leaders and educators curtail the cultural collision and collusion that is occurring within their schools? This is the paramount question that educators and school leaders must ask themselves.

It is difficult to offer resolute prescriptions with regard to curtailing the suspension and expulsion rate among Black male students; however, if there is to be any achievement in this area as well as a reduction in the number of Black male students choosing to end their compulsory education, there has to be a moratorium placed on the *business-as-usual model*. Unfortunately, what undergirds the *business-as-usual model* deployed by many educators is that there doesn't seem to be any cognitive dissonance as it relates to the plight of Black male students, especially from the inner city (McCray, 2008). The Merriam-Webster dictionary defines *cognitive dissonance* as when a person has "a psychological conflict from incongruous beliefs and attitudes held simultaneously." Thus, *cognitive dissonance* occurs when a person encounters a situation that strongly goes against the person's previously held views. This, in essence, creates anxiety within the individual, and thus, the individual usually accepts the *cognitive dissonance* as truth and reality, or works tirelessly to undo the current situation in order for it to align more with his or her original perception. The problem many educators and school leaders face in regard to young Black male students is that the crisis among Black males has become the expected norm. There doesn't seem to be any *cognitive dissonance* as it relates to the excess number of Black males who are suspended and expelled from school, which results in them being underemployed as well as unemployed and eventually finding themselves part of the criminal justice system (Wilson, 2009). In order for such a *lack of expectation* of Black males to be reversed, educators and school leaders should begin thoroughly critiquing the assumptions that are embedded within school practices that impede the progress of Black males.

The Challenge of Today's Savvier Students

There is a process taking place in our inner city schools that is impacting young Black males to a significant degree. This process is operationalized on two levels. On the one hand, educators and school leaders recognize that today's students are savvier (e.g., technology) and more sophisticated (e.g., relationships, world view, awareness, etc.) than previous generations of students (Nisbett, 2009; Wagner, 2008). Thus, a sentiment among some is that today's students are more like adults in many respects, and it is crucial for educators to accept this notion and figure out a way to educate them with regard to students' specific inquiries, views, and opinions. Although this is seen as a challenge for educators, nevertheless, something positive is reserved for those who bring an enormous amount of social capital with them to school (i.e., the *schoolboys from the burbs*). For these students, educators make a conscious effort to employ strategies that will accommodate their *adult personas*. On the other hand, the *adultification* process that is taking place in our schools as described by Ferguson (2001) in her research is the process that involves educators seeing *adultified* young Black males in the most negative way possible. Ferguson (2001) found that these students are also savvier and more sophisticated in politics, relationships, and community and school issues; however, this sophistication is usually displayed via the *code of the streets* (Anderson, 1999) and the *code of shady dealings* (Wilson, 2009; Venkatesh, 2006). And because they bring little cultural capital to school with them, and their education is undergirded by the *correspondence theory* (which will be explained in-depth later in the chapter), any sign of adult motivations shown among them is deemed not worthy of attention and considered a *grave threat* to the school's culture.

Such sentiments by educators can lead to an incredible amount of discrepancies in the discipline process between the *good bad boys* from the *burbs* and the *good bad boys* from the *hood* (Black, 2004; Cartledge, Tillman, & Johnson, 2001; Casella, 2003; Keleher, 2000; Mosca & Hollister, 2004; Raffaele-Mendez, Knoff, & Ferron, 2002; Skiba & Peterson, 1999). Educators' and school leaders' perceptions of their Black students as having adult motivations and being willfully bad is one of the main reasons why there seems to be an academic as well as a discipline gap (Gregory & Mosely, 2004). Researchers (Gregory & Mosely, 2004; McCray & Beachum, 2006; Raffaele-Mendez et al., 2002; Thomas & Stevenson, 2009) have consistently found that students of color (particularly Black males) tend to be disproportionately affected in a negative way when it comes to school punishment.

Misconceptions of Black Male Behavior

McCray and Beachum (2006) lamented that an argument could be made that Black male students misbehave in school more than other subgroups and, thus, are on the receiving end of more punitive measures from educators and school officials. However, Skiba and Knesting (2001) opined emphatically that researchers who have studied the intersection of race and discipline have found no evidence that Black students act up at a considerably higher rate than other ethnic groups. "Furthermore, these same authors [Skiba and Knesting] stated that black students are the recipients of 'harsher' disciplinary consequences and for 'less severe offenses' than their white counterparts" (Skiba & Knesting, 2001, p. 31, as cited in McCray & Beachum, 2006). Also, other researchers arrived at a similar conclusion with regard to the notion that Black students are no more devious than other ethnic groups (Thomas & Stevenson, 2009; Skiba et al., 2002). These researchers found no evidence that Black students engaged in more serious disciplinary infractions; in fact, they discovered patterns of differential treatment of Black students for office referrals, especially stemming from subjective classroom-level situations (Fenning & Rose, 2007; Ferguson, 2001; Noguera, 2003; Skiba, Michael, Nardo, & Peterson, 2002; Thomas & Stevenson, 2009).

The notion that Black male students willfully misbehave is operationalized through the subjective judgments educators and school officials make when it comes to administering punishment to students. This results in some alarming statistics. According to Day-Vines & Day-Hairston (2005), in the U.S. today, Black students represent 16.9 percent of the student population, but they account for 33.4 percent of all school suspensions (Thomas & Stevenson, 2009; U.S. Department of Education, 1999). Thomas and Stevenson (2009) also found that 71 percent of all disciplinary infractions and referrals can be attributed to boys. They went on to opine that "a closer analysis shows that African American boys represent a disproportionate percentage of boys overall who are subjected to exclusionary disciplinary action. The overrepresentation of African American boys in school discipline referrals and exclusionary consequences has been well documented since the 1970s" (p. 165).

Impact on Achievement

Unfortunately, not only is there a discipline gap concerning young Black boys, but there is an achievement gap that exists as well. Undoubtedly, the discipline gap intersects with the academic achievement of young

Black boys. According to Jackson (2008), while young Black males consist of 9 percent of the student population, they consist of 20 percent of the number of students enrolled in Special Education classes that offer services to the low achievers and *mentally impaired*. The corollary is that young Black males only represent 4 percent of those individuals in the *gifted and talented programs* (Thomas & Stevenson, 2009). It is worth noting that attributing adult motivations to young Black males seems to be streamlined with the disciplining of them, as well as the labeling of them as mentally impaired. Ferguson (2001) made it abundantly clear in her research that young Black boys stand the risk of being labeled as *mentally retarded* or *mentally impaired* as a result of the negative *adultification* that is applied to them in school.

The labeling of young Black boys as *mentally impaired* as a result of their behavior was solidified in 1994 when the American Psychiatric Association declared that misbehavior was connected to a certain type of disorder (Ferguson, 2001). As Ferguson (2001) notes, "The willingness to label youth behavior as a mental disorder places more emphasis on the individual child's mannerism (i.e., *youth pathology*) and neglects relevant cultural and social issues that come with such mannerism and style" (p. 195). According to Ferguson (2001), *Oppositional Defiant Disorder* (ODD) was the official clinical name given to youth who were perceived as misbehaving. Youth who are prone to be labeled as ODD are those youth who exhibit a "negative," "defiant," "disobedient," and "hostile" behavior over a six-month period toward authority figures (Ferguson, 2001). Today, there is indeed an overrepresentation of Black students, especially young Black boys, who are labeled as *mentally retarded* and *emotionally disturbed* (Skiba et al., 2006). The National Research Council (2002) also found that Black students are more overrepresented than their European counterparts in the categories of *mentally retarded* and *emotionally disturbed* (as cited in Skiba et al., 2007). In fact, Parrish (2002) found that in just about all 50 states, Black students are far more overrepresented in the categories of *mentally retarded* and *emotionally disturbed*.

It is entirely plausible that once students have been labeled with ODD, it is a painless effort for educators and school officials to brand these students as *mentally retarded* and *emotionally disturbed*. Skiba et al.

(2006) found in their research that discrepancy was more likely as the disability grouping became more subjective. If Black male students are not allotted the privileges of being young, but instead are treated with the same expectations as adults where there is little room for the *good bad boy* image to play out, then it is reasonable that such perceptions are leading to more discipline referrals, including more referrals into special education (i.e., where services for the learning disabled, emotionally disturbed, and mentally retarded are offered). Indeed, the National Research Council (2002) did discover that classroom management skills played a role in the discrepancy of referrals by educators. Skiba et al. note:

> African American students with poor anger control were more likely to be placed in more restrictive settings [special education placement]. Such results are consistent with other research showing that classroom teachers may differentially interpret the behavior of African American students as threatening or confrontational, and that teacher skill in classroom behavior management is a clear sense of minority disproportionality in special education. (p. 421)

The notion of arbitrarily labeling young Black boys as *mentally retarded* or *emotionally disturbed* is troubling. At the very best, this impression is haphazard, random, and messy. And at the very worst, this notion of placement and referrals of Black male students is insidious with a sinister undertone. In the pipeline of young Black boys' education, it seems as if it goes something like this—from the classroom to the principal's office, and then on to suspension and expulsion; from suspension and expulsion, on to becoming a high school dropout, and then on to prison. At the very best, it seems the special education placement of young Black boys represents a halfway house where they do their time waiting for what seems to be their prophetic and inevitable educational journey.

Cultural Pluralism Is Needed in Schools

One of the impediments for school success among Black males involves the structure of the school culture and climate. The lack of cultural pluralism that exists within the school culture is what McCray (in press) believes partly undergirds the obstacles that many Black males face in the educative process. Carter and Warikoo (2009) proffered that "culture is characterized by shared values, beliefs, behaviors, styles, and tool kits of symbols, stories, rituals, and wrong views" (p. 368). Carter and Warikoo went on to indicate that culture is also the "practices ranging from speech style and language to specific kinds of physical interaction, to taste in music, clothing, and food and other symbolic ethnic ques" (p. 368). Thus, according to Ward Goodenough, "Culture consists of whatever it is one has to know or believe in order to operate in a manner acceptable to its members . . ." (as cited in Keesing, 1974, p. 77). As was indicated in this chapter as well as previous works (Beachum & McCray, 2004; Beachum & McCray, 2008), the culture for many young Black male students undoubtedly has an impact on their educative experience (Ferguson, 2001; Wilson, 2009). Many Black male students who come from impoverished communities have very little in common with their school's culture (Ferguson, 2001; Wilson, 2009). And most of the adults in the school who are given the task of educating them are from middle-class backgrounds, live outside the community, and are usually of a different ethnicity (Haberman, 2005; McCray, Wright, & Beachum, 2006). Thus, it places many Black male students from the inner city in a very peculiar situation of total conformity to a culture they already perceive as nonmalleable, and in some instances hostile, with regards to who they are and where they come from (Lakomski, 1984). Black male students, especially those who are labeled as *troublemakers* with little to no social capital, are keenly aware of the power differential between themselves and the adults. This awareness is exacerbated when class is also used as a tool to undergird power differences (McDermott, Raley, & Seyer-Ochi, 2009; O'Connor, Hill, & Robinson, 2009; Thomas & Stevenson, 2009; Wilson, 2009).

Finding a New Pedagogical Paradigm

The aforementioned power differences that exist in inner city schools are embedded in the pedagogical ideologies of educators and school officials. Thus, educators and school leaders should also begin to unsubscribe to the antiquated *correspondence theory* (Bowles & Gintis, 1976), which implies that "school children…are infinitely malleable and passive creatures upon whom the inescapable processes of schooling impress those norms and dispositions required of them in the work place" (Lakomski, 1984, p. 152). There is no doubt that one of the purposes of schooling is to prepare children for the economy of the 21st century; however, it seems educators, and especially policymakers, over the past 20 years have engaged in fanaticism with regard to how to educate the *poor* and students of color. It seems as if everyone is at the table of the *poor and student of color educational development* except for the poor and students of color themselves. It is extremely naïve to not surmise that this power differential has not trickled down from policymakers to school districts (i.e., educational leaders and educators) and to the parents and students themselves.

As noted at the beginning of this chapter, statistics concerning young Black boys are dire. School officials are doing a disservice to the communities they serve, as well as the nation, by continuing to subscribe to an antiquated *correspondence theory* that calls on students to be passive cultural vessels with nothing to add. This pedagogical engagement has proven not to work, especially in the inner city. Nevertheless, many schools continue to engage in such a pedagogical approach (e.g., direct instruction) and are determined to eradicate the school's culture of the *troublemakers* who do not conform to the school's formal or informal curriculum. The problem with this *just crusade* is that, in many cities, the dropout rate among minority students is hovering around 50 percent (Alexander & Entwisle, 2001; Cosby & Poussaint, 2007). Our public schools and policymakers must drop the *moral idealism* act and begin to realize that there is an entire generation of young people being lost because the concept of cultural pluralism is null and void in many of our schools (McCray, in press).

Options for Young Black Males

With the lack of *cultural pluralism* within the school's culture and the school's strict adherence to pedagogical ideologies such as the *correspondence theory*, many Black males are left vulnerable. They are now faced with the decision of conforming to a school's culture—a culture they perceive to devalue them because of their race and class status—or rebelling (i.e., leaving the *game* with some form of dignity). These are options that school officials can ill afford to continue to present as viable choices. Lakomski (1984) proffered that students from low-wealth-community and minority groups whose cultures might clash with the school's culture go through a progression of unconscious decision as it relates to conformity and nonconformity. Lakomski (1984) also indicated that there are behaviors that students employ when faced with the decision whether to conform or not to conform to the school's values and beliefs. Lakomski (1984) pointed out that the first behavior involves conforming. The students receive the explicit values and beliefs of the school and choose to conform without the slightest trauma. This choice to conform is usually put into practice by those who are already closely aligned with the school's culture. Ferguson (2001) labeled these individuals in her research *schoolboys* because they bring with them to the schoolhouse gate the cultural capital needed to succeed academically and socially. The other behaviors put into practice consist of the explicit values and beliefs of the school being received and believed by the student; however, there are other contradictory messages that are bombarding the student. Thus, Lakomski (1984) indicated that these students experience a *cognitive dissonance* and choose to employ one of three specific behaviors. First, the *troublemakers* (Ferguson, 2001) choose not to play the *game* at all and instead opt to play their own game. Second, the *schoolboys* recognize the *game* and what it takes to succeed and, thus, develop a behavior style that will allow them to win the *game*. This set of *schoolboys* (i.e., *schoolboys from hood*) is different from the *schoolboys* (i.e., *schoolboys from the burbs*) who experience little to no *cognitive dissonance* within the school's culture. This group, from middle- to elite-middle-class families, brings an enormous amount of cultural capital with them to school. The *schoolboys* from the inner city bring only a small amount of cultural capital to school with them; they come from working-class families who are adamant about them following the explicit (i.e., formal) rules of the school (Ferguson, 2001). Finally, the last behavior put into practice by those who experience *cognitive dissonance* involves what Lakomski calls complete confusion that results in "'craziness,' other serious mental disorders, and even suicide" (p. 157).

The insidious part about Lakomski's prescriptive behaviors by students is that there are school policies and structures put into practice by educators and school officials to overtly usher out of the *game* or *diagnose as crazy* those who do not follow the *explicit* rules of the *game*. The problem is, the rules are not always explicit and it is not a *game* for those students, particularly young Black boys, who one day might find themselves underemployed, unemployed, suicidal, or in prison (Cosby & Poussiant, 2007; Wilson, 2009). Along with those *schoolboys* who have decided that they will play the *game,* even the Black *schoolboys* who bring immense cultural capital to school are at risk of crossing over to the *troublemakers'* side (DeCuir-Gunby, 2009; Ferguson, 2001; Warikoo & Carter, 2009).

The *crossing over* has been the subject of much debate with regard to Black male achievement. The concept of *crossing over* is primarily centered on the notion of what many scholars see as pressure from peers to shift from the *schoolboy* image to the *troublemaker* image, or from the *good good boy* image to the *good bad boy* image (Cosby & Poussaint, 2007; Ferguson, 2007; McWhorter, 2001; Noguera, 2003; Ogbu, 2004; Patterson, 2006). However, other scholars see the notion of *crossing over* as a corollary of the dysfunctional, biased, and oppressive culture that all too often is quick to label all Black boys' behavior as *being willfully bad (i.e., having adult-like motivation)*s well as suspect (Beachum et al., 2008; Ferguson, 2001; Noguera, 2003; DeCuir-Gunby, 2009; Warikoo & Carter, 2009). Nevertheless, it is paramount that a debunking and unearthing of the reasons why some young Black males choose to take on the *troublemaker* or *good bad boy* persona occur. A comprehensive examination must also critique how schools are choosing to deal with the young Black boys who are labeled as *troublemakers* or *good bad boys*. As previously noted, this type of labeling often occurs as a result of attributing adult motivations to young Black males; in other words, believing they are willfully bad. Thus, it is critically important for educators and school officials to understand how they are reacting to young Black males in their schools.

Finding Common Ground for Solutions

In order for the issues that are impacting young Black males from the inner city to dramatically dissipate, educators and school officials need to have a better understanding of the *culture collision* and *collusion* that is happening in their schools. As indicated at the beginning of this chapter, "It takes two to make a thing go wrong." And the education that many minority students and students from the inner city are receiving has gone awry. This crookedness that is producing such inequity and inequality amongst a generation of young Black males must be appropriately addressed by all stakeholders. Educators and school officials can no longer place the blame solely on students and their community. Many educators and school officials have refused to capitulate to research that debunks the antiquated *correspondence theory* that places the malleability solely on students when it comes to schooling. This lack of malleability (i.e., inadequate cultural pluralism, non-culturally responsive pedagogy, and non-culturally relevant leadership) on the part of educators and school officials is a critical mistake. This lack of malleability among educators and school officials is the foundation of the *collusion process.* In essence, the *cultural collision* that is happening in many of our urban schools is undergirded by educators embracing the *correspondence theory* that requires students (especially young Black males) to become passive vessels in the learning process. When it comes to achievement and increasing students' aptitude, research has been explicitly clear that students are curious individuals, and today's culture of video games, iPods, movies, music videos, sophisticated sitcoms, and the like has enhanced their inquisitive nature even more (Nisbett, 2009). And when this inquisitive notion intersects with the *code of the streets* and the *code of shady dealings* that many youth bring to school, it calls upon educators to be cognizant of such intersectionality and adjust their pedagogy accordingly.

To curtail the high dropout rate that is occurring in many of our inner city schools, educators and school officials must become more mindful of their role in the *collision* process. School leaders should seriously consider implementing equity audits within their schools with regard to the discipline gap (Skrla et al., 2004). Such equity audits are designed to critique the school to determine if any inequity exists within the school as it relates to teacher equality, programmatic equality, and achievement equality (Skrla et al., 2004). According to Harney (2001), it is crucial that educational leaders correct the dropout rates among students of color. Harney proffered that achieving equity in this realm is just as critical as closing the achievement gap. This undergirds the notion that educators and school leaders can't begin to address the achievement gap if the students are not in the classroom. As the literature has shown (Ferguson, 2001; Gregory & Mosely, 2004; McCray & Beachum, 2006; Thomas & Stevenson, 2009), there seems to be a positive correlation between students who receive a lot of referrals to the principal's office as well as suspensions and expulsions with those who eventually drop out of school. Black males seem to be overly represented in each of these categories (Ferguson, 2001; Gregory & Mosely, 2004; Thomas & Stevenson, 2009). Thus, for there to be a dramatic dissipation in the dropout rate among Black boys, school leaders must address the discipline gap. This will entail educational leaders using equity audits to ascertain useful data in a spirit of ethic of critique (Starratt, 2004). This includes the number of referrals, suspensions, and expulsions that are happening within their schools, and whether there is a serious discipline discrepancy among the student population.

But such critiques and audits must go beyond the data. Educators and school leaders also must begin to address other serious issues that might be exacerbating the discipline gap. These issues include concerns as to whether students feel empowered (Banks, 2001) within the school's climate and culture (McCray, Alston, & Beachum, 2006). Ferguson (2001) indicated that students are well aware the first time they walk into the halls of the school whether it is a place that values who they are and where they come from. Such empowerment for students of color, especially Black males, ceases to take place in concert with the deficit thinking among educators (Solorzano, 1997) as well as the adultification of students (Ferguson, 2001). Such deficit thinking among educators is operationalized with their view that students of color and students from the inner city are inherently flawed, suspect, and corrupt, and thus have nothing of value to offer or contribute to the learning process. This is also the link that leads to the *correspondence theory.* And, unfortunately, these students do not engage in the persona of the *good good boy* and instead take on certain *good bad boy* characteristics. When this happens, educators and school leaders are all too willing to carry out the *collusion* of the *cultural collision* and begin to usher such individuals out of the education process and out of a life of fulfillment.

Conclusion

The archenemy of the discipline gap that has been referred to in this essay is one of caring. It is imperative that an ethic of care (Starratt, 2004) is a part of a school's culture and climate. On many occasions quasi-liberal school officials and educators deliver exhortations in the school's mission statement that the caring of students is embedded in the school's curricula (i.e., school culture). Unfortunately, this rhetoric seemingly never becomes operationalized within the daily activities and duties of the school's educators and leaders (i.e., school climate). It seems, in many instances, just the opposite of an *ethic of care* is being carried out via the *deficit thinking of teachers, application of correspondence theory,* and the *assignment of adult motives on student behavior.* For caring involves being committed to the students, regardless of where they come from and who they are (Starratt, 1991). According to McCray, Alston, & Beachum (2006), caring involves affirming who the students are with respect to their cultures but "providing corrective feedback to the students when they are behaving inappropriately" (p. 15). Thus, corrective feedback does not entail attributing adult motivation to student behavior and thus creating an educational pipeline where students can go from the classroom to the prison cell. In our view, this is anything but an ethic of caring.

Chapter Five

From Notions of "Acting White" to Thug Theology

The Impact on Adolescent Black Males' Educational Achievement

In 2002 the U.S. Congress passed the No Child Left Behind Act, which mandated that American schools eliminate the gap between the social classes and between minority groups and whites by 2014. I don't know if most members of Congress actually believed that such accomplishments are possible. But if so, they are deeply ignorant of the forces that operate to produce high academic achievement. Intellectual capital is the result of stimulation and support for exploration and achievement in the home, the neighborhood, and the schools

(RICHARD E. NISBETT, 2009, P. 119)

In this chapter, we explore the issue of academic engagement with regard to adolescent Black males. As was stated in chapter four, Black males seem to be the most vulnerable subgroup population in our society (Fletcher, 2007; Wilson, 2009), ergo, we once again focus our attention on them in this chapter. Such a lamentation seems oxymoronic, considering we now have our first Black president of the U.S. Unfortunately, this notion is operationalized in a simple exercise that is conducted in one of our classes. Each semester in one of the diversity classes we teach, students are asked to imagine that in each corner of the room there is a specific personality: a gay White male, a White female, a Latino woman from a low socioeconomic bracket, and a Black male. The students are then asked to proceed to the corner of the personality they feel experiences the least amount of discrimination in our society. The purpose of this exercise is to show how discrimination comes in many different forms. Nevertheless, the students must make a decision out of the four choices that are presented to them. Admittedly, each personality in each of the corners is subject to some form of discrimination. The gay White male is subject to discrimination due to his sexual orientation, even though he is White and a male. The White female is also subject to discrimination due to her gender. No one can argue that the Latino woman from a low socioeconomic background is not subject to harassment and social injustice. And, of course, the Black male's problems within the U.S. have been well documented. That said, each time the exercise is conducted, there is hardly anyone who proceeds to the corner of the Black male or the Latino woman from a low socioeconomic background—the reason: it is just too much of a risk. There was a deduction on our part that with the election of the first Black president, more students might proceed to the corner of the Black male in this exercise and attempt to make an argument that Black males have finally arrived, considering the U.S. is presently being led by a Black man. Alas, even in this triumphant period for American progress and race relations, the exercise still produces similar results.

The Plight of Black Males

Achievement Discrepancy between Black Males and Females

When one looks closely at the statistics associated with Black males, it is certainly understandable why the students in the aforementioned exercise might be hesitant to choose the corner of the Black male. Black males, today, in these tough economic times have some of the highest unemployment rates than any other group (Cosby & Poussaint, 2007, Wilson, 2009). Cosby and Poussaint also found that "Young black men are twice as likely to be unemployed as white, Hispanic [Latino], and Asian men" (p. 9). Out of all the ethnic men (i.e., White, Latino, Asian), Black men are the only men who have a higher unemployment rate than their female counterparts (Wilson, 2009). It seems as if the Patrick Moynihan report still holds some validity. In 1965, Senator Moynihan issued a warning to the Black community and society as a whole that Black males were not keeping up with Black females with regard to high school completion as well as higher educational attainment. He indicated at the time that such discrepancies between Black males and females could have devastating consequences for the Black family as a whole. According to Nisbett (2009), at the time of the Moynihan report, "Black females were 30 percent more likely to graduate from high school than black males" (p. 102). Professor Nisbett has also found that, today, Black females are twice as likely as Black males to have an IQ over 120.

As we highlighted in previous chapters, when Black males do not graduate from high school with at least an adequate education, their opportunities are severely limited. Ergo, other illicit opportunities seem more attractive and eventually lead to death, homicide, or imprisonment for many (Venkatesh, 2006). Cosby and Poussaint (2007) have found that homicide is the leading cause of death for Black men between the ages of 15 and 29. By the time Black males have reached their thirties, 60 percent of those who have dropped out of school have spent some time in prison (Wilson, 2009). Thus, Pettit and Western (2004) have asserted that "Among [black] male high school dropouts the risk of imprisonment [has] increased to 60 percent, establishing incarceration as a normal stopping point on the route to midlife" (as cited in Wilson, 2009, p. 72). In the previous chapters, we lamented that many of the problems related to Black males can be ameliorated by attaining a thorough and sufficient education. Black males who go on to finish high school as well as college have substantially higher potential over those individuals who choose not to complete high school or attend college (Cosby & Poussaint, 2007; Ferguson, 2001; Nisbett, 2009; Shelby, 2005; Wilson, 2009). Harvard professor and sociologist, William Julius Wilson, has found that Black males are not keeping pace with Black females with regard to attending and graduating from college. He acknowledged that within most ethnic groups, women tend to "exceed men in college completion" (Wilson, 2009, p. 66). But according to Wilson, "This discrepancy is particularly acute among African Americans, and the gap has widened steadily in the past twenty five years" (p. 66). Today, for every 100 bachelor's degrees earned by Black men, 200 bachelor's degrees are earned by Black women (Wilson, 2009).

Cultural Factors Influencing Black Males

Our attention now turns toward cultural factors that may be prohibiting young Black males from achieving academically. This is an issue that has been researched and discussed by a wide variety of scholars (Cosby & Poussaint, 2007; Ferguson, 2001; Ferguson, 2008; hooks; 2004; McWhorter, 2001; Nisbett, 2009; Noguera, 2003; Ogbu, 2003; Patterson, 2006). For the most part, there has been inaction from many scholars with regard to problematizing the intersection of the culture of young Black males with academic achievement (Patterson, 2006; Wilson, 2009). Patterson opines:

> The main cause for this shortcoming [emphasis on cultural issues] is a deep-seated dogma that has prevailed in social science and policy circles since the mid-1960s: the rejection of any explanation that invokes a group's cultural attributes—its distinctive attitude, values and predispositions, and the resulting behaviors of its members—and the relentless preference for relying on social factors like low incomes, joblessness, poor schools and bad housing.

No one can deny that the history of Blacks in this country has been one of "stalled progress" (Ferguson, 2008). Scholars (i.e., Dyson, 2003; Quarles, 1987; West, 1993; Wilson, 2004) have written numerous articles and books in which they have documented the historical struggles Blacks had to endure ; struggles that have been undergirded by structural issues (i.e., implicit as well as explicit racism, segregation, poor schools, and severe psychological damage). In fact, we have alluded extensively to some of these structural struggles in this book. And we do recognize the importance of contextualization. For without the contextualization and problematization of a social phenomenon (i.e., the underachievement of Black males), scholars as well as laymen can engage in what social psychologist call *the fundamental attribution error*. This occurs when individuals fail to problematize the behavior of individuals within the social or situational circumstance and move readily to attribute the behavior of such individuals to a personality or character flaw. Thus, the purpose of this chapter is to try to take an equilibrium approach with regard to the dire state of affairs many adolescent Black males are finding themselves in. Nevertheless, we caution that this balanced approach, with regard to Black males' student achievement, is juxtaposed with some of what has already been written in the earlier part of the book.

Revisiting the Notion of "Acting White"

The dilemma facing young Black boys and their educative experience has been labeled and coined in a variety of ways in recent years. One of the most common notions in the literature, with regard to Black student achievement or lack thereof is the notion of *acting White*, a term coined by Fordham and Ogbu (1986). According to DeCuir-Gunby (2009), "The label of acting white is given to someone when they engage in behavior that is considered 'white'" (p. 115). DeCuir-Gunby found that Black students are very cognizant about presenting themselves as *authentically Black* and could easily decipher between those activities deemed as White and those that were deemed as Black. DeCuir-Gunby found that:

> Since being Black is very important to African Americans, engaging in a "white" activity is somewhat insulting to the Black community. For instance, students frequently get the label of *acting White* when academically successful. There are some African Americans who do not view academic achievement as characteristic of Black; academic achievement is seen as a white activity and students who are academically successful are often seen as *acting White*. (p. 115)

Fordham (1986), in her work "Black students' school success: Coping with the 'Burden of Acting White'" talked about how many Black students face the possibility of being accused of *acting White* if they show signs of rigorous academic curiosity. Ogbu (2003) also discovered similar findings in his study. Ogbu observed Black students in a wealthy suburb and found that their cultural outlook often slowed down their achievement when compared to White students.

For those Black students who are not able to perform what Lacy (2007) has called *script switching*, they are at risk of losing on the academic front as well as the *authentically black* front. According to Lacy (2007), script switching is where Blacks change their entire demeanor as they move between mainstream institutions and other Blacks. On the one hand, there is the need to prove to the mainstream that they belong in whatever position or place that Blacks have not historically been represented in (i.e., in a particular school, a certain neighborhood, a high-end department store, etc.). Thus, the concept of acting White is undergirded by the notion that Black students have made an implicit decision that they would prefer to lose on the *academic front* instead of losing on the *authentically Black* front (Fordham & Ogbu, 1986). Tyson, Darity, and Castellino (2005) found that acting White could be based on the premise that high academic achievement was not for Blacks. Tyson et al. (2005) reported that "black students striving for academic success have their cultural authenticity as Blacks called into question and are accused of acting white" (p. 584). Therefore, there is also a greater need to prove to other Blacks that they are *authentically Black* (DeCuir-Gunby, 2009; Fordham & Ogbu, 1986). This includes style of dress, walk, handshake, style of music, and unfortunately many times capitulation to academic engagement (Cosby & Poussaint, 2007; Decuir-Gunby, 2009; Ferguson, 2001; Fordham & Ogbu, 1986; Lacy, 2007; McWhorter, 2000; Patterson, 2006). The notion of acting White was manifested to the mainstream when at the 2004 Democratic National Convention, then Senator Barack Obama indicated the following concerning Black student achievement: "children can't achieve unless we raise their expectation and turn off the television sets and eradicate the slander that says a black youth with a book is *acting white.*"

The notion of *acting White* has been called into question by many scholars, and scholars of color in particular (see O'Connor, 1997; Spencer et al., 2001; Tyson et al., 2005). One of the most prominent studies that attempted to debunk this notion was by Tyson et al. (2005). In their study, they concluded that Black students' attitudes were not entirely different from their White counterparts' when it came to academic achievement. They conducted an in-depth study of students in North Carolina for over a year and a half concerning Black students' attitude and dispositions with regard to academic achievement. They reported that in only one of the eight schools they studied was there any indication of the notion of acting White among the Black students. According to Tyson et al. (2005), "Contrary to the burden of acting white hypothesis, the black students in this study who avoided advanced courses did so for fear of not doing well academically" (p. 599). They went on to indicate that the students' decision to not take advanced classes was a result of them being sensitive to the issue of their grades suffering if they did not do well. Tyson et al. found fault with Fordham and Ogbu's (1986) *acting White* theory due to the fact that Fordham and Ogbu did not take into consideration that "high achievement (either racialized or class-based oppositionality) may be a common experience in some schools in which high-status groups are perceived to be privileged in placement and achievement" (pp. 599–600). In other words, Tyson et al. proffered that the notion of academic disengagement and anti-intellectualism desultorily occurs between Black and White students.

Regardless of whether the concept of *acting White* is a legitimate assumption or simply a meretricious notion with regard to Black male student achievement, then Senator Obama might not have been too far off the mark in his exhortation concerning Black students being accused of acting White if they engaged in high academic pursuit. Neal-Barnett (2001) acknowledges that Black students do differentiate between what they consider as White activities as opposed to authentically Black activities. Alas, some of those activities that are considered White activities are activities that would make one successful in life's endeavors. Neal-Barnett (2001) found that some Black students were likely to find speaking Standard English and being placed in advanced classes as White activities, and thus, unpalatable. Also, Neal-Barnett found that the list of White activities went beyond academic achievement to include style of dress. Students were considered acting White if they purchased their clothes from Gap and Abercrombie & Fitch instead of dressing in Tommy Hilfiger and FUBU.

What's up with the Cool Pose?

Tyson et al. (2005) made it clear in their study that they found little evidence in the eight schools they studied that Black students were opposed to high academic achievement. We also find it somewhat problematic to subscribe to the notion that Black students go to school on a daily basis with the explicit desire of learning as little as possible. But a crucial point to be examined is that Black females are doing better academical-ly than Black boys (Nisbett, 2009; Thomas & Stevenson, 2009). In the pre-vious chapters of this book as well as the first part of this chapter, we provided compelling statistics indicating that Black boys may be falling behind not only their White and Asian counterparts but also Black females. Throughout this book, we have talked about an array of struc-tural issues that are impacting Black boys in the educative process. But a critical question that must be asked is to what extent Black boys are being pernicious with their own academic success and careers by engag-ing in what Orlando Patterson (2006) coined "a poverty state of mind." Even though Black males may have every intention of going to school to perform, a critical inquiry concerns whether the potential conflation of hip-hop culture with the "cool pose" is having devastating conse-quences on their educative experience.

This conflation of hip-hop culture and the well-entrenched cool pose seems to have garnered the attention of others in the Black community as well. It was disheartening to hear on a semiurban radio show one evening the dialogue between a radio talk show host, his co-host, and a renowned scholar. These three individuals set out that evening with the best intentions of trying to engage the listeners in the art of writing. In fact, the host of this particular show makes an effort nearly every after-noon to convince his audience to pick up pen and pad and become writers. Thus, on this particular evening, the host asked the renowned scholar and his co-host why Black boys are not engaged in the art of writ-ing? It was at this point that the co-host, whose main job is to provide comedic relief from time to time, lamented "don't you have to know how to read before you can write." It was not the co-host's comedic axiom that was distressing, but it was the sense of realism in his statement that was so poignant. Of course, the co-host's statement is not applicable to all young Black males, regardless of how the media tries to portray them. But nevertheless, there does seem to be a certain anti-intellectu-alism or anti-academic engagement that is connected to Black masculin-ity within some pockets of the Black community (Dyson, 2005). We should clarify here that the terms intellectualism and academic engage-ment, although brothers in inquiry, are somewhat nuanced. Indeed, intellectualism carries a connotation of in-depth inquisitiveness that directly connects with political, social, and economic issues of society. And while academic engagement is critically important, especially for young students, one might argue that it is a prerequisite for intellectual inquiry. An even more insightful avowal in the exchange between these three individuals on air that evening consisted of the comments made by the renowned scholar. The scholar articulated that these Black boys are not stupid. They listen to the radio. They hear the lyrics that glorify thug life and downplay intellectualism. The scholar went on to indicate that they hear Ciara's flow articulating "I tried that good boy game/But the dope boyz turning me on. . . .." Unfortunately, the conversation between the scholar, host, and co-host quickly pivoted to another topic. As great as the host and the co-host are with this particular show, a wonderful opportunity was missed to unearth the notion of whether the most vulnerable and fragile segment of the Black male population has taken the "cool pose" to an entirely different level that glamorizes "thug life" (more on this later in the chapter) with the corollary being an adverse impact on their educative experience where academic engagement is placed to the wayside in pursuit of other endeavors.

Cool Pose minus Posterity

The term "cool pose" was originally coined by Majors and Billson (1992) to help understand the mannerism and style many Black men engaged in on a daily basis for a number of reasons. According to White and Cones III (1999), "In a society where lingering manifestations of racism continue to restrict life's options and prevent the achievement of goals, many African American males have adopted a coping style called 'cool pose'" (p. 91). White and Cones III delineated exactly how the "cool pose" is carried out. According to White and Cones III, the "cool pose" consists of "physical postures, clothing style, social roles, and social scripts, behaviors, style of walk, content and flow of speech, types of dances, and attitudes that are used to symbolically express masculinity" (p. 91). Unfortunately, in concert with the rising popularity of rap music, gangsta rap in particular, the cool pose went from a coping mechanism with regard to racism to a hyper-masculine way of life for many young Black adolescents. Ironically, the very strategies that many Black adolescents and young men used to cope with the daily struggles of living in America evolved into problematic nihilistic dispositions that are in many ways adversely affecting their chances at long-term goals such as educational attainment, emotional stability, as well as career satisfaction. Most people who study the cool pose agree that it is almost a rite of passage for most Black boys (Cosby & Poussaint, 2006; Ferguson, 2001; hooks, 2001; White & Cones III, 1999). Alas, in many instances, this prerequisite for Black boys as it relates to masculinity is having devastating consequences for their opportunities in middle-age adult life. White and Cones (1999) sum it up rather succinctly, "As a coping mechanism, cool pose can be adaptive and maladaptive. Obsessive reliance on its symbolism can lead to negative consequences. First, in the long run, exaggerated, ritualistic masculine facades, postures, and poses cannot substitute for real educational and occupational achievement" (p. 93).

The "ritualistic masculine facades" and "postures" that White and Cone III (1999) are referring to are not only devastating in Black males' education and occupational achievement, but could also have a destructive impact on their future generations. As was indicated earlier, Nisbett (2009) has found that there is an increasing separation between Black male and Black female academic achievement, which could exacerbate Black female/male relationships by adversely impacting young Black males' Romantic Market Value (RMV). Relationship guru Larry Davis has found that individuals are chosen as potential mates based on their RMV, which include a host of criteria. One of the criteria that is embedded in the RMV consists of having a good paying job or career. A hyper cool pose where overdependence on facades, postures, and poses adversely impact educational achievement can, in an oxymoronic way, jettison the very individuals who are seen as cool in young adulthood from the marriage pool (Cosby & Poussaint, 2007; Nisbett, 2009). According to Nisbett (2009), "The unwed mother rate is 72 percent for blacks, compared to 24 percent for whites" (p. 101). Nisbett also conveyed that "This statistic represents a host of problems for black children, not least of which is that the poverty rate for single-parent homes is far greater than it is for two parent homes. Perhaps equally important is the fact that such homes have only one adult, and the fewer adults there are, the less stimulating is the environment" (p. 101). Cosby and Poussaint (2007) have also indicated similar concerns with regard to Black male/female relationships.

The increasing educational gap between Black men and women can create covert fissures among the sexes. Collins (2005) has found that Black men who have been left out of the educational arena as well as mainstream employment opportunities have used their sexual prowess toward Black women to overcompensate for their miseducation, under-employment, unemployment, and increasing marginalization. According to Collins, "In this context sexual prowess grows in impor-tance as a marker of Black masculinity....Black women become reduced to sexual spoils of war, with Black men defining masculinity in terms of their prowess in conquering . . ." (p.151). Collins's depiction of young Black men who are unemployed/underemployed and miseducated and who dwell in urban areas is powerful in contextualizing the *hyper cool pose* many young Black males capitulate into masquerading.

Is Hip-Hop and Rap Music a Culprit?

Undoubtedly, in the world of hip-hop, the issue of sex conflated with materialism and violence seems to manifest in young impressionable Black males. Tupac, an iconic figure in the rap industry, manifested this rap trinity in his final album, *The Don Killuminati: The 7 day theory*. In his second cut, called *Hail Mary*, Tupac, under the alias Makaveli proclaimed "I ain't a killer but don't push me/revenge is like the sweetest joy next to getting p****." Thus, if Tupac could only manifest two out of three in this particular song (i.e., sex and violence), Notorious B.I.G. definitely highlighted the role of sex and materialism in some of his cuts. In his song, "Big Papa" Notorious B.I.G. indicated ". .you'll find me back in the club, mackin h***/my crew's behind me...mad question askin/blunt passin, music blastin/but I just can't quit cause one of these honies [females] Biggie gots to creep with/Sleep with. . . ." In this particular verse of Notorious B.I.G.'s lyrics, he is talking about a lifestyle that involves clubbing, sexual prowess, and marijuana usage. Likewise,

Tupac in his verse expressed the sentiments that the only thing better than revenge was sex.

Even though *gangsta rap* seems to have dissipated somewhat over the years, lyrics by rap artists that place sexual conquest as paramount in the lives of Black men still remain prominent in today's hip-hop and rap songs. And since these lyrics do not involve killing the police or drive-by shootings, they seem to be seen as less execrable and more palatable, with regard to not doing physical harm to mainstream society. The corollary of violence in rap and hip-hop lyrics subsiding is the diminution of the counter push from activist to regulate music. Nevertheless, such aforementioned lyrics are still having a devastating impact on young Black males' disposition and outlook on life (Stewart, 2004; Brown, 2006) At the very least, such lyrics provide implicit guidelines (Brown, 2006) to young Black males, especially those from impoverished communities and without fathers, on how to conduct themselves with regard to masculinity.

It is critical to point out that male hip-hop and rap artists are not the only ones who provide instructions to young Black males on what is considered cool and masculine. In many instances, female R&B artists provide such implicit and unofficial edicts to young Black males. If Patricia Hill-Collins is correct in her assessment concerning vulnerable young Black males' esteem and self-value being connected to the display of their sexual prowess, the prerequisite for such an endeavor potentially does even greater harm to young Black males than the act itself. There are a plethora of female R&B artists who have embedded in their lyrics the ideal male as it relates to masculinity and being cool. For instance, the group Destiny's Child made a song in 2004 entitled, "Soldier," where they talked about the kind man they preferred. Kelly's (one member of the dynamic trio) verse flowed something like this: "We like them boys [who] eyes be so low from that chiefin [smoking marijuana excessively]/I love how he keep my body screaming…If is status ain't hood, I ain't checking for them/Better be street if he is looking at me/I need a soldier That ain't scared to stand up for me. . . ." In these lyrics, the group, Destiny's Child, has defined what has sadly become the panacea for far too many young Black males, with regard to a *hyper cool pose*, that is negatively impacting their educational and employment opportunities. The

aforementioned verse calls for everything from having a street disposition to smoking marijuana excessively as well as being an ultimate sex
machine—hardly qualifications of a candidate for 21st century jobs.
Likewise, Ciara in her song, "I like your thug style," professed "You
changed the game/I like your thug style when I'm around you/you
always make me smile…make me so excited. . . ."

These verses by the late and talented Tupac and Notorious B.I.G., the
group formerly known as Destiny's Child, and Ciara, are only a few of
the lyrics that have young vulnerable Black boys and girls dancing and
humming at any given time. Such lyrics implicitly tell young Black boys
how they must act in order to be considered cool and masculine. And
likewise, such lyrics implicitly tell young Black girls the ideal male who
is worthy of her consideration and time. Nevertheless, there are many
Blacks who will insist that such lyrics do not adversely impact them. In
their study, Franklin and Rasheed (2004) have found that there is a pre-
vailing notion that the lyrics in music are not the culprit for the destructive behavior among many young Black males. We concede that lyrics
in of themselves are not the sole cause of many of the problems young
Blacks encounter. Nevertheless, to not interrogate lyrics that solely focus
on misogyny, violence, sexual promiscuity, and an emphasis on getting
rich by any means necessary with regards to potential culpability would
be negligent. We believe to capitulate to the notion that such lyrics do
not have an impact on the minds of young adolescents is dangerous.
And if this notion is indeed true (i.e., music does not influence adolescents), then stakeholders and shareholders should demand that marketing departments be dismantled as a result of unnecessary overheads, and
companies should be held accountable by their stakeholders and shareholders for business malpractice and spending billions of dollars each
year on advertising. This, of course, is not going to happen because the
bottom line is marketing and advertising work! Thus, companies go to
great lengths to target certain segments of the population, adolescents
in particular, to ensure their products sell (Davis et al., 2009; Thrasher et
al., 2006). And we do not believe it to be a huge stretch to compare marketing campaigns to the influence music has on adolescents, and in
many cases adults. In fact, scholars such as Mickel and Mickel (2002)
maintain that music goes beyond the call to purchase a certain item;

music in many instances fills both psychological and physical needs. Brown (2006) has found the following:

> Music has the power to move the listener toward an alternate reality. Harmonious musical beats accompanied by emotive lyrics can almost create an inviting escape to an abstract paradise of the listener's choice. On the one hand music can take a listener to a distant past memory while on the other hand music can stimulate a listener to entertain ideas of whatever unrealized fantasies she or he may prefer (p. 50).

Likewise, Shusterman (2005) proffered that "Hip hop captures its fans not simply as music but as a whole philosophy of life, an ethos that involves clothes, a style of talk and walk, a political attitude, and often a philosophical posture . . ." (p. 61). There is no doubt that many Blacks have used music in the past to escape the U.S.'s harsh realities with regard to racism and the ills that came with it. Music genres such as blues and rhythm and blues (R&B) have always historically had a coping message with regard to enduring the form of bigotry and prejudice the U.S. had to offer (West, 2004). But the difference in this historical coping mechanism of music in contrast with some of today's music is that there were few calls on Black men to resign or capitulate to thug life (Shusterman, 2005) as well as Black women to yield themselves as sexual objects. In the plethora of lyrics that allude to such aforementioned pathology and constantly receive radio air rotation, it has, unfortunately, generated informal rites of passage for young Black boys and girls.

From a Hyper Cool Pose to Thug Theology

Over the last few years, it seems that the cool pose has morphed from Majors and Billson's depiction of a certain type clothing, speech, and walking style to something a little more provocative, at least in name. The new terminology that is now being used in Black barber shops and has become part of the Black lexicon is the phrase, *thug*. On any given day when one patronizes a Black barber shop where Black men congregate for grooming and to discuss the latest issues of the week from sport, politics, community issues, as well as relationships, it is almost a given that the discussion will evolve into how many young Black adolescents have become fixated on the concept of *thugism*. Here we are using the term *thugism* to refer to young Black males who are engaged in a defiant and antagonistic revolution toward the system as a whole under the auspices of self-defense and class rebellion (Dyson, 2001). These are the young men who feel as if they have been left behind by the educational and financial systems and must resort to achieving wealth and status by any means necessary—many times engaging in illicit financial activity. Dyson (2001) has alluded to *thugism* or *thug theology* as the conflation of extravagant materialism and defiant hedonism—both reinforcing the other. According to Dyson (2001), "Thug ambition is unapologetically predatory, circumventing the fellow feeling and group solidarity demanded of revolutionaries" (p. 64). In an oxymoronic way, the very structures that young vulnerable Black adolescents would like to change are reinforced even more due to their predatory ambition.

Even though there are differences of opinions to the degree to which *thugism* and *thug theology* is obstructing young Black males' success, we purport that is quite dangerous for a generation of young Black males to not only embrace such lifestyles but also make it synonymous with masculinity. In many instances, thugism and thug theology have become the new version of *cool*. It is no longer sufficient for young Black men to embrace one another with a common handshake, as well as know the latest dance moves, or walk and talk a certain way; the ante has now been raised to potentially achieving materialism through illicit means to satisfy hedonistic pleasures. In the meantime, such endeavors are helping to contribute to an entire generation of young Black boys being left behind educationally and economically. Hip-hop artist Drake explains this exploration for success in his latest song, "Successful." In this particular song, Drake talks about what being successful requires. He laments "I want the money, money and the cars, cars/and the clothes, the h*** I suppose/I just want to be/I just want to be successful." Undoubtedly, there will be many young Black boys who will achieve instant financial status for a short period of time through illicit means and predatory ambition. There will also, undoubtedly, be those who achieve permanent success through certain predatory methods while pivoting toward more licit and socially acceptable means of earning power. It would certainly be inaccurate to perceive that this type of activity is only limited to vulnerable young Black adolescents; certainly, these type of actions, where individuals use illicit means and predatory ambition to achieve wealth and status, can be found in every race, ethnicity, and class strata in the U.S. Nevertheless, the problem is exacerbated when these choices seem to be the only options available to a select group (i.e., young Black boys) as a result of economic and structural circumstances (Wilson, 2009) as well as the glorification of the lifestyle. As we have indicated, much has been discussed with regard to the economic and structural issues that lead some young and vulnerable Black adolescents to embrace *thugism* and *thug theology*. But not nearly enough attention has been focused on how this lifestyle is embraced by not only Young Blacks from low-wealth communities but also young Blacks from middle-class and elite Black communities.

There has been anecdote after anecdote in Black conversation regarding young Black males from middle-class and elite Black communities who engage in the emulation of thug behavior. We referred to this type of emulation earlier in the chapter as script switching. This pattern of behavior occurs as a result of the ever-increasing blurred lines between being cool and thug behavior. Both are synonymous among certain Blacks as being masculine and authentically Black. Undoubtedly, there will be many Blacks who will deny that they associate the *cool pose* and *thugism* with Black male masculinity as well as being authentically Black. Indeed, the overwhelming majority of Blacks, especially middle-aged ones, deplore the behavior of Black males who, unfortunately, capitulate to *thugism* and *thug theology*. Even Black men who once subscribed to such behavior and managed to escape this lifestyle intact from an emotional, spiritual, financial, and educational standpoint are also quick to point out that such behavior is counterproductive. And for young Black men who are from middle-class backgrounds, the acquiescence to *thugism* and *thug theology* can have devastating consequences on their future aspirations in life. But for some reason, a generation of young Black adolescents have become fascinated with the ideas and values associated with *hyper cool pose* and *thug theology*. Indeed, many young Black adolescents, historically, have always subscribed to a cool disposition, but never at the cost of their intellectual fortitude.

Thus, where is the call for young Black boys to engage in serious intellectual endeavors? It seems that the call has been suppressed with a plethora of insidious overt and covert pathological depictions of what young Black adolescents should aspire to become. This suppression has not only come in the form of racial, economic, and structural waves, but such suppression of the call for intellectual curiosity can also be found within certain segments of the Black community. Thus, we proffer here that the calculus of academic disengagement among Black male adolescents combined with the notions of *acting White* to *hyper cool pose* and *thug theology* are keeping many of them from achieving their fullest potential.

A Call beyond Urban Normalcy

Thus, a critical question regarding Black male adolescents' role in our society centers on our expectation of them. Unfortunately, it seems that Black males are being asked to engage in everything except for rigorous academic engagement that produces skill sets for 21st century jobs. It seems that the ultimate panacea for Black males, even in the 21st century, is one of entertainer or athlete. This was something that President Obama alluded to when he spoke at the 100th anniversary of the National Association for the Advancement of Colored People (NAACP) convention. President Obama told the audience the following:

> They [African American children] might think they got a pretty jump shot or a pretty good flow, but our kids can't all aspire to be LeBron or Lil Wayne. I want them aspiring to be scientist and engineers, doctors and teachers, not just ballers [basketball players] and rappers. I want them aspiring to be a Supreme Court justice. I want them aspiring to be the president of the United States of America.

President Obama's remarks were very poignant concerning the trajectory of many young Black males, especially from the inner city. The unofficial *rites of passage* that many young Black males from urban and low-wealth communities must spend an enormous amount of time cultivating involves excelling on the football field or basketball court; cultivating a *mouth piece* that gives them *street creditability* with women as well as hours of practice in hopes of becoming the next hip-hop and R&B sensation. This whole notion of *street creditability* is what the group

Destiny's Child was referring to earlier in this chapter. Edward P. Jones (2007), a notable Black author and winner of the Pulitzer Prize for fiction, summed it up this way. Today, for many Black males,

> Scholars come close to being freaks and some students with poor grades no longer strive, no longer care. Perhaps that is what happens to a people who worship potty-mouthed rap stars with the belief that dying for 50 cents is a step upward, a people who worship the new golden calves called bling bling, a people who worship men known only for shooting and bouncing balls up and down a wooden floor. (p. xii).

The quandary that many Black males face as it relates to engaging in intellectual rigor is nothing short of a quagmire. It is a pervasive setup on multiple fronts from the beginning, and only the ones with enough cultural and social capital and the benefit of two family households (Nisbett, 2009) stand a legitimate chance of navigating through this maze of mixed and misguided messages. On one front, there is the implicit message being delivered by mainstream society via mass media to Black males that they are put on this earth for the sole purpose of entertaining and performing. This view of Black males is an extension of the once held view that Black males were indeed placed on this earth to serve—a subservient class of people (Shelby, 2005). During the era of slavery, Black males were placed on auction blocks and examined for their physical attributes, while Black women were inspected for their child rearing potential (Jordan, 1968). Black men were viewed as thoroughbreds designed specifically to bring in profits for slave owners (Jordan, 1968). It was considered the highest crime for Black men or women to learn how to read or write. As slavery came to an end, it was not an accident that many Black men pivoted from serving White slaveholders to becoming entertainers. Such careers were attractive and allowed Black men to escape in many instances from back-breaking labor and cotton fields where the profits were little or none and work was all too familiar. Today, it seems that for many young Black men, entertainment and athletics are the first line of defense for making a living, and careers undergirded by education are a fallback alternative, if a viable option at all. We do not want to give the impression that there is anything wrong with young Black adolescents striving to become entertainers and athletes; after all, these careers can be very lucrative. But the reality is that there are only so many openings/slots in the world of athletics and entertainment. For a young Black male adolescent to focus solely on becoming the next T. I. (an Atlanta hip-hop artist) or Kobe Bryant at the expense of becoming an engineer, doctor, teacher, etc. is extremely dangerous and all too often a trajectory of failure.

The other front that is having a devastating impact on young Black male adolescents is the implicit message that is coming from within their own communities. This message involves the unspoken notion concerning intellectual endeavor and inquiry. Earlier in this chapter, we talked about the notion of *acting White* and the research that has been conducted that supports the theory as well as the research that has tried to debunk it. Even if the notion of *acting White* is outdated and antiquated, which we do not believe it is entirely, a serious inquiry has to be made into the notion of the hyper-cool pose which can lead to anti-academic engagement and anti-intellectualism. Young Black boys are being bombarded by explicit as well as implicit messages via music from hip-hop and R&B that to engage in serious intellectual endeavors is a sign of weakness and a threat to masculinity. It seems that the roles that were assigned to Black men during and after slavery, which is that Black men were placed on this earth not to engage in intellectual inquiry but to become ultimate sex machines (i.e., the reproduction of off-springs for slaveholders) is subconsciously being played out in a way that is having a devastating impact on their chance of making a decent living. Michael A. Fletcher, a *Washington Post* reporter, asked "What does it mean to be a black man?" He went on to give a compelling scenario with regard to three hypothetical young Black boys entering kindergarten at the same time to convey the dire situation that is facing many young Black males adolescents. According to Fletcher (2007), the statistics reveal a portrait of where one of the young boys ends up in prison, while the other young boy is on the verge of dropping out of school. Lastly, the third young boy is on a trajectory toward high academic pursuits. There is no doubt that the structural issues of the school and school culture have a major role in this ominous set of events concerning young Black boys' academic achievement (Wilson, 2009). And we have discussed these issues in depth throughout this book. But a serious and earnest critique of the unofficial *rites of passage* that young Black boys are explicit-ly and implicitly encouraged to go through via the media and within their own communities must be open for discussion and part of the cal-culus if the plethora of problems confronting Black males are to dissipate over the next decades.

When young Black boys spend their time perfecting entertaining as well as athletic and sexual prowess as a result of a *dangerous illegitimate rite of passage*, there is hardly anytime left for serious academic engage-ment and inquiry. Alas, "fewer than half of black boys graduate from high school four years after entering the ninth grade" (Fletcher, 2007, p. 5). In fact according to Chaddha, Wilson, and Venkatesh (2008), "The urban graduation rate is only 34.6 percent compared to a suburban graduation rate of 81.5 percent…a gap of 47 percentage points" (p. 83). Thus, we believe that the conflation of structural and cultural solutions will yield the most positive results for academic achievement among young Black males.

A Paradigm Shift for Young Black Males

With the election of the first Black president, Barack Obama, many in the Black community saw an opportunity to provide a paradigm shift for young Black boys with regard to their perceptions of what they can aspire to become. Indeed, the election of President Obama can move the pendulum from young Black boys aspiring to become rappers and *ballers* to those wanting to become engineers, doctors, teachers, and sci-entists. It should be pointed out that *White collar* professional role mod-els did exist within the Black community at one point. But with the massive exodus of individuals who were doctors, engineers, and busi-nessmen from the once class mosaic community (Shelby, 2005), such pro-fessions became less attractive for many young Black males (Wilson, 2009). The tenor of this specific chapter is that *white collar* professions, which require concerted academic engagement, are seen by many Black males as less masculine as opposed to the skill sets needed to cultivate and perfect balling on the basketball court and developing a *mouth piece* for rapping and smooth talking. One argument for this phenomenon is that as middle-class and elite middle-class Blacks started to move out of predominately Black communities, it left a vacuum for many low-wealth Blacks with regard to the great possibilities they could achieve and strive for (Shelby, 2005). In other words, the role models (i.e, doctors, engineers, lawyers, and bankers) for high achievement were just not prevalent to provide a bifurcation (Gines, 2005) of Black masculinity.

In order for this paradigm shift of what it means to be a young Black male in the 21st century to take hold, there have to be concerted efforts to debunk the false binary ways of thinking within some segments of the Black community of what it means to be a Black male (Taylor, 2005). According to Taylor, for far too long the love for hip-hop culture has been one of the barometers with regards to whether someone is authentically Black. Gordan (2005) also has found that "Hip Hop has…become a primary exemplar of authentic black culture" (p. 105). Gordan goes on to posit that "this development [authenticity of blackness] is attested to not only by the multitudes of black adolescents [but] folk in their twenties and thirties (and even older) who are drawn to it in their quest for an authentic black identity" (p. 105). Taylor (2005) proffered that although hip-hop culture originated in the Black community on the streets of Brooklyn and is embraced by a wide spectrum of Blacks, it is disingenuous to assume that every Black male or female should have an unyielding affinity for hip-hop. To many, these words may be interpreted as blasphemy. Undoubtedly, there will be many who will lament that such an exhortation is simply a resignation of those who have not done well in perfecting the balance of *script switching* from a high achieving student to a cool, hip-hop regurgitating future buppy (Black urban professional). The dichotomy that exists now in many segments of the Black community is one that delivers an exhortation that hip-hop combined with Black Entertainment Television (BET) are the CNN of Black culture. And if you are not getting your cultural cues from these venues, something must be wrong, and you are not authentically Black (Taylor, 2005). The problem is, from a cultural standpoint, (we certainly acknowledge that there are substantial structural issues with these problems) this bifurcation of what it means to be Black is oxymoronically having a devastating impact on Black males, and as a corollary the Black family.

When the type of binary way of thinking mentioned above becomes pervasive and seemingly invisible within a community, it can help produce (with the help of racist and bias structural arrangements) a plethora of young Black men who drop out of school, a substantial rate of crime within the Black community, a disproportionate number of Black men incarcerated, and imbalances between the sexes that impact potential marital rates as well as productive posterity (Beachum & McCray, 2008; Kitwana, 2002; Kunjufu, 1993). And the distressing part about this is that there doesn't seem to be any cognitive dissonance to these issues facing young black males (more on this in Chapter 7). The binary thinking that subscribes to the notion of *acting White,* where if you study hard or are interested in activities that have not been approved by the *Black authenticators,* has to be debunked. For it is disingenuous for Blacks with substantial social and cultural capital and benefactors of the *notion of acting White* to wage a judgmental campaign on the most vulnerable in the community who can also benefit from the "so-called" *acting White* descriptors (i.e., studying hard, diversifying ones' interests, and becoming an avid reader). In other words, there is a certain segment of the Black community who is engaging in duplicity. On the one hand, they level criticism to those who are not engaging in *authentically Black endeavors* (i.e., listening to certain genres of music, dressing in a certain style, employing a certain lexicon, and cultivating a familiarity with an overall hip-hop urban lifestyle); however, these same individuals (i.e., those with social and cultural capital) were given the skills to engage in the *authentically Black culture* while also perfecting and cultivating skills needed to succeed in White society. The problem is that the majority of Blacks (e.g., two-thirds of Black children are born in poverty) are not equipped to master the *script switching skills* that are needed to succeed in an adolescent deployed culture (Gordon, 2005) and the greater society.

If hip-hop culture and all that comes with it represents Black culture, as the great Chuck D once proffered on the CNN (Taylor, 2005), a counter narrative must be provided regarding other mediums (*channels)* where Black students can receive different cultural cues. We believe it is a mistake for young Black adolescents to interpret that Black culture can be authenticated from one perspective. Therefore, it is critical for educators as well as the community to debunk the myth that Black culture is represented in its totality through the combination of hip-hop, BET, *a hyper cool pose*, and *thug theology*. Educators and school leaders must think outside the box and be creative in showing young Black male adolescents that Black culture consists of much more than what they see on Black Entertainment Television and the lyrics that bombard them continuously on the radio.

Conclusion

We have readily acknowledged that there are substantial structural issues that continue to plague the educative process of young Black males. And it should be pointed out that Professor William Julius Wilson has found in his research that when it comes to academic achievement, the recalibration of structural issues plaguing inner city youths yields a better return rate than the modification of cultural issues (Wilson, 2009). In other words, according to Professor Wilson, when structural issues (i.e., the dissipation of redlining, influx of business to urban communities, better schools and teachers) are adequately addressed, youth, and people in general tend to do a lot better. Having said this, educators and school leaders have considerably more control over embedded problematic structural issues within the school than the culture that many urban students from low-wealth communities are exposed to. Thus, it is a mistake for educators to concede to the notion that learning and academic achievement cannot take place due to the aforementioned problematized edifying that occurs among many inner city Black youth. It is our desire that this chapter will accomplish just the opposite by arming educators and school leaders with cultural knowledge and awareness to adjust their leadership and pedagogy to inspire academic achievement and intellectual curiosity. But we caution that such inspiration cannot take place as long as educators and school leaders refuse to engage in earnest dialogue with students about the implications of the notions of *acting White*, the *hyper cool pose,* and *thug theology,* as well as the importance of hip-hop and rap as the Black cultural authenticators.

Undoubtedly, many young Black youth from the inner city will subscribe to the notion of *acting White* as well as the *hyper cool pose* and *thug theology*. They will also declare rap and hip-hop music as their Black CNN. We proffer that it is educational malpractice by school leaders and educators to not engage this thinking and cultivate their own cultural awareness to provide compelling counter narratives. This entails educators and school leaders' pedagogy going beyond literacy and numeracy if there is to be a drastic reduction of the number of young Black boys who are placed in special education and labeled mentally impaired, as well as the reduction in the percentage of Black boys who are suspended and expelled from school with the gateway being underemployment, unemployment, and imprisonment. In actuality, the cultural issues we have referred to in this chapter intersect with the structural components of the school—vis-a-vis teacher and student interaction. If educators resign to the notion of engaging students' culture in a constructive manner, then our cultural collision ultimately comes to fruition with the corollary being the sabotaging of academic achievement and life chances by both educators as well as the students themselves. If this is not a structural issue, then we do not know what constitutes a structural issue. In order for young Black males who are experiencing a cultural collision in urban schools to achieve academically, school leaders and educators must begin to take ownership of their role in the cultural collusion.

Chapter Six

Hip-Hop vs. the Schools

Educators' Perceptions of the Impact of Hip-Hop Culture on Students

Hip-hop allows a kind of marriage between the rhetorical and the musical by means of some of the most amazing linguistic virtuosity we have seen in the English language.

— CORNEL WEST (WEST, 2008, P. 123)

Great rhetoric has lost its sway as noble verbal art has been replaced by the mindless redundancy of themes we're all too familiar with: women, weed, wine, cars, and jewelry. The thug persona has replaced skillful exploration of the thug's predicament: hustling in a culture where crime is the only option of the economically vulnerable. Beyond questions of craft, there's the archetypical rap record executive who's more interested in releasing records by artists reveling in rims rather than rhymes, and in breasts and behinds more than setting young brains on fire with knowledge of their people's plight.

— MICHAEL ERIC DYSON (DYSON, 2007, P. 148)

In its short existence, hip-hop music has been embraced worldwide by youth, pummeled in the media for supposedly increasing social misery (i.e., promoting violence, drug use, salacious sexual imagery, and mindless materialism), and hailed as a significant musical breakthrough. Hip-hop culture has transcended musical boundaries and now impacts

speech, clothing, mannerisms, movies, web sites, television programming, magazines, and energy drinks (Dyson, 2007; Kitwana, 2002). It is
quite apparent that hip-hop culture has the ability to impact and influence youth (Beachum & McCray, 2004; Kitwana, 2002; Kunjufu, 1993).
Part of its awesome power could also be its position as a partially post-
modern form of self-expression (Dyson, 1997). In other words, hip-hop
culture is characterized by diversity, change, flux, improvisation, and creativity. Conversely, most U.S. schools still operate in a very 20th century modernistic manner, meaning that they are often rigid, stagnant,
and/or slow to change The problem may not be so much that the schools
are failing, but that they have become obsolete in many ways (Wagner,
2001). In fact, it is not so much the schools themselves that are obsolete,
but rather how some of the teaching strategies and the way the learning
process have been organized. The reality in schools is largely shaped by
the educators (teachers and administrators) who work diligently with
students (Berelson & Steiner, 1964; Kunjufu, 2002; Starratt, 1991). What
happens when the perceptions of these educators differ from those of
students? Who gets to define school reality (Starratt, 1991)? "Given the
salience of hip-hop culture in the lives of many urban American youth,
the educational community has begun to pay considerable attention to
the pedagogical possibilities of hip-hop culture within formal schooling
contexts" (Hill, 2009, p. 2). It is here we begin with our inquiry. The purpose of this brief study is to examine educators' perceptions of hip-hop
culture.

Relevant Research

The following is an overview of relevant research as related to hip-
hop/rap music, hip-hop culture and studies/scholarship, youth/pop-
ular culture, school culture, and the perceptions of educators.

Hip-Hop/Rap Music

Hip-hop/rap music emerged out of the unique experiences of urban
youth of color. In its early years, it was commonly known as simply rap
music, but it evolved into what we now call hip-hop music. Some schol-

ars connect hip-hop to the larger musical experiences of Africans in the diaspora (Gilroy, 1993; Keyes, 2002). Many would agree that its actual birthplace was in New York City in a postindustrial context (Kitwana, 2002; Rose, 1994; West, 2008). Kunjufu (1993) illuminated the origin of the term when he wrote, "Hip-hop is a term derived from an early New York rapper named 'Lovebug Starski'" (p. ii). Rose (1994) asserted, "Hip Hop is a cultural form that attempts to negotiate the experiences of marginalization, brutality, truncated opportunity, and oppression within the cultural imperatives of African American and Caribbean history, identity, and community" (p. 21). Similarly, Dyson (2007) wrote:

> The origins of rap are black and Latino. And it wasn't simply a matter of African American youth, but black folk throughout the diaspora. DJ Kool Herc came over from the Caribbean, transporting with him that booming sound system that was common in particular spaces in West Indian culture. That revolutionized and reshaped the sonic landscape in the Bronx, the birthplace of hip-hop. It was here that the four central elements of hip-hop emerged: break dancing, DJ-ing, graffiti, and rapping (p. 72).

Of the central elements that have securely stood the test of time, DJ-ing and rapping are still alive and well. Hip-hop has gone from a form of music at the margins of society, embraced by what some would call outcasts, to the center of much musical discussion and heavy musical rotation on radio stations and constant airplay on computers, CDs, and iPods. In addition, it has broken the barriers of music and now encompasses much more. Hip-hop/rap music has now spawned what can be called hip-hop culture.

Hip-Hop Culture

The contemporary hip-hop experience is now much more than just music. Hip-hop culture is vast, diverse, and dynamic. Kunjufu (1993) agrees, "Hip-hop is a highly dynamic culture whose very nature is change" (p. ii). Au (2005) notes that hip-hop music has gone from primarily rapping, break dancing, DJ-ing, and graffiti to including linguistic expression, beliefs, mannerisms and demeanor, and fashion. Today, hip-hop culture has hyper-exposure with hip-hop-related terminology regularly appearing in mainstream television programming, hip-hop-themed kids' shows like *Hip-Hop Harry*, hip-hop-themed magazines and web sites, and even award shows dedicated to hip-hop music (e.g., the Source Awards). Now, hip-hop culture has even crossed national boundaries, influencing legions of youth in other countries (Dyson, 2007). Kitwana (2002) noted the irony of increased global exposure when he stated:

> Rappers' access to global media and their use of popular culture to articulate many aspects of this national identity renders rap music central to any discussion of the new Black youth culture. The irony in all this is that the global corporate structure that gave young Blacks a platform was the driving force behind our plight...As everyday people worldwide struggle to survive, these corporations [today's mega-corporations] work diligently to sell them a slice of modern life—from automobiles and electronics to food and entertainment (p. 11).

Therefore, hip-hop culture has expanded, even exploded, but at what cost? We must also recognize hip-hop culture's awesome power to influence the values and behaviors of today's youth and especially Black youth (Beachum & McCray, 2004; Kunjufu, 1993).

Hip-hop culture has captured the hearts and minds of large numbers of today's youth. This influence has the potential to be positive or negative, but there has been a steady concern with regard to the more negative aspects. These include an overemphasis on material gain, extreme violence in lyrics, the encouragement of misogynistic behaviors, glamorization of selling drugs and prison culture, and the promotion of aggressive and/or antisocial behaviors (Beachum & McCray, 2008; Dyson, 1997; 2007; Gause, 2005b; Kunjufu, 1993; West, 2008). In the past, youth, especially Black youth, looked to their families, churches, and schools in order to develop and cultivate their values (Guy, 2004; Kunjufu, 1993). "Today, more and more Black youth are turning to rap music, music videos, designer clothing, popular Black films, and television programs for values and identity" (Kitwana, 2002, p. 9). "The ages between 13-17 are when they [teenagers] are particularly vulnerable to outside influence and before their values and ideas are fully developed" (Kunjufu, 1993, p. 81). Therefore, Black youth are especially vulnerable to influences during their critical teenage years and at the same time they can be bombarded with messages and images from different outlets (i.e., music, videos, Internet, magazines). It is imperative for concerned adults to delve deeper into the worlds of youth, including hip-hop culture. Ginwright (2004) asserted, "Hip-hop culture is central to conceptualizing black youth identity because it is an essential pathway to understanding their struggles, realities, and possibilities" (p. 34).

Hip-Hop Studies/Scholarship

Hip-hop has increasingly become the subject of academic study and curricular innovation over the years. Originally, much of the work focused on the impact of rap music's lyrics on youth (Hall, 1998; Took & Weiss, 1994; Tyson, 2002). Hill (2009) wrote, "Although this research provided critical and nuanced rejoinders to the moral panic of the day, the narrow focus of the studies ignored issues of culture, identity, and power with regard to youth engagement with hip-hop" (p. 4). Thus, the overemphasis on cause-and-effect approaches overlooked other crucial dimensions of why hip-hop culture is so magnetic and how youth make meaning of hip-hop in their lives. Petchauer (2009) reviewed hip-hop educational research and categorized the early research into three kinds of literature. They are historical and textual literature, social commentary literature, and grounded literature.

Three significant literatures have characterized hip-hop studies over the last 15 years. Historical and textual literature was one of the first approaches used to analyze hip-hop. Many of these works were conducted by academics or activists on hip-hop-related themes and on youth as the subject of their research. These works include works on social history (Rose, 1994), interdisciplinary thought (Dyson, 2004), African diaspora connections (Thompson, 1996), cultural studies (Giroux, 1994), and analysis of values (Kunjufu, 1993) to name a few. Although these works were necessary and foundational, they still lacked a voice that spoke directly from the hearts and minds of youth most directly involved with hip-hop. Petchauer (2009) agreed:

> Broadly, they have helped to establish hip-hop as an essential domain of inquiry and identified some of the complex and contradictory ways that these texts could function as both oppressive and empowering. Despite the valuable

and creative contributions, they are often limited to researchers' explanations of how hip-hop might function in the lives of those who create it in local contexts...Scholarly works are separate when they focus on products such as rap songs more than the groups, processes, and contexts that create them (p. 950)

Thus, the limitations of historical and textual literature opened the door for social commentary literature.

Social commentary literature was generated beyond the walls of academe and thus had a broader appeal to a much wider audience. These works provided a unique perspective of authors closer to the world of hip-hop while at the same time providing additional critique (see Dyson, 1997; George, 1998; Kitwana, 2002). While these works provided a more balanced perspective of hip-hop and brought readers closer to the genre, it also unearthed new areas of concern. "Although social commentary works are vital contributions to documenting and understanding hip-hop, they do not allow one to evaluate conclusions through a critique of chosen techniques of data collection and analysis, all of which are necessary for replication and evaluation of the validity of the arguments and interpretations presented" (Petchauer, 2009, p. 951). Therefore, while these works appeal to more people, they typically lack a suitable amount of research rigor and deeper analysis that enhances explanation and intertwines similar and sometimes disparate bodies of literature. Grounded literature was proposed as a way to reconcile the weaknesses in the previous two approaches.

Grounded literature places more of the focus on those who live, develop, and immerse themselves in hip-hop. Scholars and social commentators (and journalists) speak from a privileged position, many times removed from the real experience of youth and how they understand hip-hop. Some of the grounded literature includes Clay (2003), Duncan-Andrade (2008), and Hill (2009). The grounded approach often originates from those closest to hip-hop or it at least makes their experience paramount, unlike historical and textual approaches. "Because grounded explorations are normally directed toward an academic audience, a reader is often afforded enough methodological specificity on which to make a critical evaluation of the research findings and attempt to replicate studies, unlike social commentary approaches" (Petchauer, 2009, p. 952). While grounded literature now seems to best capture the experience of those closest to hip-hop, historical and textual and social commentary still have a place in the examination of hip-hop culture, music, and related topics. The method used may very well depend on one's purpose, audience, and intent.

Youth Culture and Popular Culture

Popular culture has become increasingly important in the lives of today's youth. Youth popular culture can be defined broadly as "the various cultural activities in which young people invest their time, including but not limited to: music, television, movies, video games, sport, Internet, text messaging, style, and language practices" (Duncan-Andrade, 2008, p. 114). Cusic (2001) asserted that there is an economic basis to popular culture, which depends on the consumption of the masses. Hall (1992) stated that popular culture is a space of contradiction in that it can reaffirm resistance or coalesce commodification. In today's society, we exist in a never-ending flood of information and technological innovations, which can serve to spread popular culture at incredible rates. An important aspect of this discussion is the ways in which youth understand and utilize popular culture. Duncan-Andrade (2008) illustrated the fact that youth popular culture covers a wide range of activities. Unfortunately, many educators are too far removed from the lives and experiences of these youth to truly grasp their perspectives. When hip-hop culture is added to the mix, there is an extra layer of misunderstanding by adults who may already harbor negative feelings about rap music (Dyson, 1997; Kitwana, 2002). Teachers and administrators would benefit from having a comprehensive view of youth that honors the knowledge they already bring to school, offers support no matter where they come from, and attempts to better understand their world and experience (including youth popular culture and hip-hop culture). Beachum and McCray (2008) explored this rationale when they wrote, "Ultimately, we endeavor to promote a critical discourse for urban school leadership, illuminating how intellectual work regarding popular culture can assist educational leaders in processing and addressing institutional practices in urban contexts. Thus, understanding the ways in which popular culture affects and infects urban youth is critical to the success of educational leaders in urban areas" (p. 102). As important as the issue of youth popular culture is the structural issue of school culture.

School Culture

School culture can impact the way in which students learn and interact with one another. Broadly speaking, "The culture of an enterprise plays the dominant role in exemplary performance. Highly respected organizations have evolved a shared system of informal folkways and traditions that infuse work with meaning, passion, and purpose (Deal & Peterson, 1999, p. 1). School culture, however, is rather unique and tied to the local communities. In addition, they "are shaped by the ways principals, teachers, and key people reinforce, nurture, or transform underlying norms, values, beliefs, and assumptions" (p. 4). During their time at school, students are expected to learn academic subjects, enhance social skills, discover ways to work with adults (i.e., authority figures), and develop good character (Beachum & McCray, 2005; Starratt, 1991; Wagner, 2001). These activities are intimately connected to the culture of a school. According to Banks (2001), "the school culture communicates to students the school's attitudes toward a range of issues and problems, including how the school views them as human beings and its attitudes toward males, females, exceptional students, and students from various religious, cultural, racial, and ethnic groups" (p. 24). Therefore, adults in schools have a major impact on the culture of their buildings. At the same time, students may bring their own cultures (collective experiences and realities) to school. The collision happens when these cultures are at odds (see Beachum & McCray, 2004). Ultimately, it is the incumbent upon educators to create healthy school environments and at the same time respect the cultures of their students. If necessary, educators also have a duty to discipline, correct, and teach students as needed if their cultural experiences are negative, harmful, or plain antisocial. Students who embrace hip-hop culture can prove to be challenging if they also develop a worldview that seems dysfunctional to educators. For example, youth who may wear their pants sagging low and overemphasize money, women, and violence (Beachum & McCray, 2008). It is up to teachers and administrators to find a way to reach any and all students who may enter the doors of their school. A positive culture in a school "amplifies the energy, motivation, and vitality of a school staff, students, and community" (Deal & Peterson, 1999, p. 8).

Teacher and Administrator Perceptions

The perceptions of teachers and administrators are incredibly important with regard to the teaching and learning process (McCray, Wright, & Beachum, 2004). Over 30 years ago, Dember (1961) asserted that perception is difficult to define and tends to be imprecise. Berelson and Steiner (1964) agreed, adding that perception is a process marked by complexity as people collect information from their interactions in the world and find ways to make meaning and interpret this sensory information. Our perceptions are also connected to how we respond and react. Thus, what an educator perceives can impact how they behave. In other words, depending on what educators perceive about a subject or their students, can directly affect their behavior (how they teach or deal with a student). Sometimes teachers and administrators have negative perceptions of some students because of their race/ethnicity or social class (Kunjufu, 2002; Beachum & McCray2004; Obiakor, 2001), which can result in these students being underserved both in overt and covert ways (Kailin, 2002; Villegas & Lucas, 2002).

Adults, in general, have disagreed with many aspects of youth culture over the years (Dyson, 1997). In some cases, this can be attributed to the generational gap and the rift between younger and older people (Kitwana, 2002). Since the evolution of rap music and hip-hop culture, it seems as if the differences between adults and youth who embrace hip-hop culture have been exacerbated. In education, it is the adults who have the most control of the educational process. If they automatically perceive a student to be predestined to failure, then there is a very good chance that the student will fail. Rosenthal and Jacobson (1968) confirmed the connection between teacher expectations and student performance. Therefore, teacher and administrator perceptions are of critical importance because it can impact their expectations and ultimately how they deal with students.

Methods

The methodology used here consisted of an open-ended survey; from that, a grounded theory approach was utilized with a constant comparative process for subsequent data analysis (Creswell, 2007; Strauss & Corbin, 1998). The surveys were distributed by email and the educators' responses were collected via email. This provided the researchers with ready-made transcripts for data analysis. Member checks in the form of follow-up phone calls provided the participants an opportunity to clarify, restate, or elaborate on certain points. Additionally, the researchers regularly discussed the methodology and findings. These crucial and candid conversations assisted us in establishing validity. These discussions were a form of peer review and debriefing for the purpose of "external reflection and input" (Glesne, 1999, p. 32). The resulting data was analyzed by utilization of the constant comparative method (Glaser, 1978).

> This procedure calls for coding data from interviews, observations, or documents under headings that appear to capture the theoretical properties of that category. Each coded category is then described as succinctly as possible to capture the meanings inherent in it. Then, using that category, all new and existing data are constantly compared to determine the descriptive adequacy of the category (Haller & Kleine, 2001).

It is important to note here that this was more of a pilot study—exploratory in nature. In essence, it gave the researchers a foundation to follow up with a larger qualitative study. Although some studies can be found on students and hip-hop/rap, there is still relatively little research on teachers and administrators and their attitudes toward hip-hop culture and its impact on the school. To fill the void of the missing perspectives of educators, an open-ended survey was distributed to a diverse group of 10 educators. Three responded to the survey. Two were classroom teachers in urban schools. One was an educational coach and facilitator (and a certified teacher and administrator). Personal data regarding the respondents appears below in Table 6.1.

Table 6.1

	Gender	Race/Ethnicity	Position	Years in Teaching or Administration
Respondent 1	Female	Black	Educational coach	12
Respondent 2	Male	Black	High school art teacher	11
Respondent 3	Male	Black	Doctoral student	N/A

The setting was a Midwestern urban school district with about 105,000 students, 229 schools, and more than 6700 full-time and part-time teachers and substitute teachers. A set of follow-up discussion questions were distributed to a class taking a course in educational leadership. The responses of both groups are analyzed in the next section.

Findings and Analysis

As a result of pilot study data collection three themes emerged. These themes included *ironies of authenticity, culture wars,* and *problems and potential.* The following is a presentation of each theme along with supporting data and a brief explanation of connections to related literature. We will elucidate two levels of analysis. On level 1, we will directly analyze data as provided by respondents with regard to corresponding theory and/or relevant research. Level 2 analysis will not only include more of the same, but will also address broader educational implications for teachers and educational leaders in the section following the findings and collection of data.

Ironies of Authenticity

In this small study, participants did discuss notions of authentic hip-hop or nostalgic reflections of hip-hop. Their comments were many times contrasted to the contemporary hip-hop so popular today. One educator commented, "I grew up with classic hip-hop, so I like 90s hip hop and some of today's songs. I am very picky when it comes to music." This person drew a demarcation between what they viewed as "classic" hip-hop and contemporary hip-hop. This same person also lashed out at the contemporary hip-hop stating, "It seems that some of today's songs lack the creativity and effort to be classified as authentic music." Another person wrote that hip-hop "had a good message at the onset/origin of hip-hop." These comments reveal that these educators recognized the metamorphosis of rap music and hip-hop culture over the years. Many can remember hip-hop's "Golden Age" when it was new, energetic, grassroots, organic, and oppositional (Dyson, 1997; 2001). Similarly, educators also sought to place hip-hop music into a sociohistorical context. One person defined hip-hop culture as an "African American renaissance of art and music beginning in the 70s that celebrates and chronicles urban living." Along this same line, another respondent stated, "I believe it to be another subculture of Black America. One that originally started in opposition to mainstream music, presenting a more real look at urban communities." These educators acknowledge a change in the music in some way and from their statements or inferences these changes were for the worst. Adults seem to have mixed to primarily negative feelings toward hip-hop culture (Dyson, 1997; Kitwana, 2002). Some of their perceptions are justified by the negative imagery that is frequently associated with the genre. Other aspects of their feelings have to do with their own nostalgic memories, which can be deceptive or instructive.

Nostalgia or aspects of collective memory can be a double-edged sword. It can lure one into thinking that the past was inherently better than the present and furthermore, things are getting generally worse. Dyson (1997) expounded upon this when he described what is known as Hegel's problem:

> They [nostalgic Blacks] often have what may be termed as Hegel's problem, named after the philosopher who believed that of all periods in history, the Zeitgeist, the world spirit, was best embodied in his own Prussian state during his life. For nostalgic true believers, it translates into the notion that the best black music happened to coincide with their own youth (pp. 131–132).

Although Dyson was discussing Black music, people do the same with other experiences, especially with regard to how they view education. In this vein, nostalgia can be problematic if it leans toward falsifying history and lacking objectivity, or becomes based in more fantasy than fact (Bissell, 2005). On the other hand, nostalgia can encourage a kind of collective memory that affirms not only one's recollection of the past, but the legitimacy of their experience. Hill (2009) agrees, "Through nostalgia, communities are able to engage in individual and collective self-critique, sustain moral traditions, and imagine a better future" (p. 112). Therefore, the educators in this study recalled legitimate memories of hip-hop music that should be placed in the proper context. As a matter of fact, during its infancy, hip-hop music was frequently dismissed and demonized. It received a fair amount of criticism, just like it does now. Thus, that "Golden Age" did not necessarily feel like one at the time, but this is difficult to realize when one is immersed in the historical moment. Educators should recognize how their past experiences can coincide with the experiences of their students and not always conflict with them. In this way, educators should examine the ways in which collective memories can help them build closer relationships with their students. Kunjufu (2002) reminds us that relationships are a key aspect of getting through to students. In addition, educators should help students understand historical context. For instance, the hip-hop challenges of today are similar to the ones faced long ago. Furthermore, these are the same obstacles faced by other musical genres. Dyson (1997) again provides acute insight:

> I'm simply arguing that all forms of Black music have been attacked both within and beyond black culture. Blues and jazz, rhythm and blues, and soul have all been viewed as indecent, immoral, and corrupting of black youth. To be nostalgic for a time when black music offered a purer aesthetic or a higher moral vision is to hunger for a time in history that simply doesn't exist...Bebop was once hip-hop. Ragtime was once rap. Bluesmen were once b-boys. What is now noble was once notorious (p. 129).

In sum, the respondents' comments were to a certain extent authentic. They should be tempered with more balanced notions of nostalgia. But the implications are not only for music or hip-hop culture; the same balance is needed as educators work with today's youth.

Culture Wars (Hip-Hop versus School Culture)

According to the responses of educators, there was a difference and a tension between hip-hop culture and school culture. Hip-hop culture largely exists within the minds, values, and actions of youth within a school. This occurs within the larger school culture that is largely created by adults (especially educators). Cultural clashes seem inevitable. One educator responded, "Students walk in hallways and sit in classes hooked up by way of iPods and cell phones to the sounds of hip-hop. I think that the accessibility of music, not specifically hip-hop, with modern technology has created counterproductive environments in school settings. Students are not focused on learning while hooked up to iPods. Students use cell phones to initiate fights and 'sex' text each other in school." Another educator remarked, "Hip hop also has a language or way of expression that counters Standard English language that is expressed in school." These comments reinforce the literature that states that Black youth especially are tuning into hip-hop music and are immersed in hip-hop culture even in school. This is obviously problematic because the majority of time in school should be spent in learning and not listening to music. The problem is that too many teachers may not be reflecting upon their own pedagogy enough to get students excited about learning academic subjects. Hill (2009) taught a progressive course to high school students called Hip Hop Literature, in which they primarily analyzed and discussed hip-hop texts (lyrics). His unique approach legitimated not only their interest in hip-hop culture, but also their lived experiences that were later unearthed during the course. Moreover, they related the themes in hip-hop texts to literary themes like allusion, signifying, metaphor, and plot (p. 22). This could be an example of culturally relevant pedagogy. This term originated with Gloria Ladson-Billings (1994) as a means of "empowering students intellectually, socially, emotionally, and politically" (p.18). She argued that culturally relevant pedagogy should include the following criteria:

1. Students must experience academic success.
2. Students must develop and/or maintain cultural compe-
    tence.
3. Students must develop a critical consciousness through
    which they challenge the status quo of the current social
    order (Ladson-Billings, 1995, p.160).

Culturally relevant pedagogy is a promising way to peak students'
interest, counter boring lessons, and connect theoretical academic concepts to the practical world of students.

The language of capitalism, commerce, and schools is Standard
English. Hip-hop culture has a tendency to generate its own unique
slang. In addition, many of these terms change depending on geographical location; thus the slang in the South is different from the slang on the
East Coast or in the Midwest. Whatever the case, it is frequently at odds
with the middle-class language expectations in American schools.
Problematic words that are popular in hip-hop culture include the "n"
word, numerous derogatory words for women, and the infamous "baby
mama/daddy." In addition, to words such as these, hip-hop tends to
relax the rules of Standard English by splitting infinitives, dropping
syllables, and cursing (usually inappropriately). Although these things
are rejected by schools, they are accepted in many local communities
where students reside (this includes Ebonics). Educators should assist
students to better grasp Standard English while not totally dismissing
their slang (which becomes a proxy for their culture). Educators can help
students learn the importance of code switching (Lacy, 2007). Landsman
(2006) expounded upon this notion when she wrote:

> We so give students little credit for what they already know: it is a primarily
> White world in places of power right now…Kids are aware of this. They do this
> kind of bidialectical work all of the time. They flip from Ebonics to street slang
> to Standard English within a five-minute period in most high schools. By ask-
> ing students to translate their work you are putting a name on what they do,
> without detracting from their home, how their grandmother or grandfather
> speaks, what their mother says when she is talking with their friends…By
> teaching these concepts, I believe that we are lessening the chaos in these ado-

lescents' lives. We are also including all the ways they speak. At the same time, we are adding to the diversity in our classrooms without denying them entry into any world (p. 226).

While on the surface it appears that the cultural clash may be the result of wayward, dismissive, or rebellious youth, it may very well reflect a deeper clash between classes. Another educator stated:

> School culture is a direct reflection of societal culture—which has always valued a white, middle class culture. So of course there is a clash between hip hop and school culture. Students are products of their environments, so their actions, behaviors, and dress are a direct result of the things valued in their community. Hip-hop is huge in urban communities, therefore, students from those communities will reflect hip hop 'attitudes.' School culture may teach you to tuck in your shirt and not to 'sag' your pants, while hip-hop displays the opposite.

This particularly insightful statement illuminates the seldom discussed class dynamic embedded in American schooling. "Class is rarely talked about in the United States; nowhere is there more intense silence about the reality of class differences than in educational settings" (hooks, 2003, p. 142). Class is also linked to the power dynamic especially in urban schools where middle-class educators have substantial power and lower-wealth students and parents have less power. These students and parents can find themselves up against huge educational bureaucracies and elitist educators who implicitly or explicitly look down on urban communities and their dwellers. According to Darder, Baltodano, and Torres (2003):

> Contrary to the traditional view, schools actually work against the class interests of those students who are most politically and economically vulnerable within society. The role of competing economic interests of the marketplace in the production of knowledge and in the structural relationship and policies that shape public schools are recognized as significant factors, particularly in the education of disenfranchised students. From the standpoint of economics, public schools serve to position select groups within asymmetrical power relations that serve to replicate the existing values and privileges of the culture of the dominant class (p. 11).

Schools can play a catalytic role in increasing class-specific differences, as opposed to the common belief that schools are actively eradicating such differences. It takes the concerted and collective effort of caring teachers and administrators to advocate for students and parents who (through no real fault of their own) cannot advocate for themselves. These educators must seek to help parents negotiate institutional "red tape," encourage and motivate students beyond their self-imposed limitations, and actively oppose policies and practices that devalue urban school students.

At the same time, the responsibility is not totally on educators—students also have a critical role to play in their own education. One educator brilliantly asserted, "Individuality seems to be the cry of many students when there is a clash between their culture and the school culture. Perhaps the best method for these students is to learn ways to adapt to their environments. They must realize that school culture is based on different values than their own, but education is the key to upward mobility and personal development. What students do outside of the school should not infringe on their activities within the school."

The Gift and the Curse (Problems and Potential)

The problems and potential of hip-hop culture places it in a peculiar predicament. The educators in this pilot study saw the obvious flaws within hip-hop culture, but also identified pockets of possibility. The negative aspects of hip-hop culture are frequently on full display on television, the Internet, and mainstream radio stations. As a result, "today, more and more Black youth are turning to rap music, music videos, designer clothing, popular Black films, and television programs for values and identity" (Kitwana, 2002, p. 9). From this we recognize the potential power of hip-hop culture to influence youth, especially urban youth of color. One of the respondents commented, "Besides the music videos that are just terrible, I have a problem with the songs themselves. To me, hip-hop always conveyed some message or had some hidden meaning." Another educator asserted, "It tends to objectify women, celebrate violence, glorify sex, and encourage civil disobedience." Similarly, another person stated that hip-hop culture was about "killings, women, and fast money." From these responses it is obvious that there are some serious negative themes in hip-hop. These problematic areas are well documented in literature with regard to materialism (Dyson, 2005; 2007), misogyny (Kitwana, 2002; West, 2008), and violence (Beachum & McCray, 2004; Dyson, 1997). Beachum and McCray (2008b) discussed the ways that these issues work together in a framework called cultural collusion. "Cultural collusion describes the negative cultural/societal implications that emerge when complex cultural cues and messages seem to influence individual and group behavior. Collusion in this case highlights the interplay among highly visible youth cultures, in this case violence, materialism, misogyny, and hip-hop culture" (p. 104). In this previous work, we suggested that educational leaders (and teachers) utilize critique, justice, and caring in their day-to-day work with urban school students (Starratt, 1991). Critique means asking deeper questions about the inequities we see. This involves becoming a more critical educator by reading diversity, equity, and social justice-related literature (see Bogotch et al., 2008; Dantley, 2002; Darder et al., 2003; Dyson, 2004; Freire, 2000; Giroux, 1997; Gorski, 2006; Harro, 2000; hooks, 2004; North, 2006; Obiakor & Beachum, 2005a; Villegas & Lucas, 2002; Young, 1990). Justice involves treating all students with a sense of fairness and being sensitive to the differences of race/ethnicity, social class, gender identity, religious beliefs, etc. Caring, as we have utilized it elsewhere (McCray, Alston, & Beachum, 2006), not only includes the obvious caring for all of our students, but also encompasses the notions of compassion, sincere dialogue, and modeling (Beachum & McCray, 2008).

While the educators cited the more glaring problems in hip-hop culture, they also identified areas of potential. One educator opined, "I love the beats and rhythm of songs; they seem to bring out different emotions and feelings associated with the music. Positive hip-hop conveys a message that listeners must try to interpret and understand." Another educator noted, "It [hip-hop culture] has become pop culture. It has been recognized and used to garner support for initiatives such as Hurricane Katrina, voting in presidential elections, and commercially sell thousands of products." From these comments we see that there is an awesome potential in the music. Any form of musical expression has the ability to solicit feelings and emotions from the listening audience. This also means that it can be used to inform, organize, and empower. An example of this is with groups like Public Enemy, a rap group from the early 1990s that was known for racially conscious and politically charged lyrics and themes. Dyson (2007) provided additional background and context when he wrote:

> They [conscious hip-hop artists] have also occasionally linked their work to quests for social justice, whether making a song to galvanize social response to police brutality or to dramatize and inspire social outrage against an unjust war. At the height of politically conscious rap...groups like Public Enemy depended on a kind of racial and political literacy for folk to grasp what they were saying (pp. 64–65).

It is this fertile area of political literacy where educators can help their students better connect their lives to world events, social history, and academic texts. Part of the problem is in the absence of political and media literacy; students can be easily lured into the seductive traps of material acquisition at all costs, hedonistic lifestyles, and unnecessary violence. Educators play a critical role in assisting their students in being able to read not only the words on pages, but also the world around them. When students begin to get a better understanding of the world, it will inevitably impact their musical tastes (i.e., they will begin to demand more from the music) and for students who create elements of hip-hop culture (music, clothing, magazines, etc.) they will do so with a critical perspective that may seek to promote more positive messages instead of negative ones.

The other critical point here is that it is difficult for positive hip-hop to flourish without being connected to a broader social consciousness or movement. The music of the 1960s was undergirded by the civil rights and Black power movements. The struggles in the streets were reflected in songs, paintings and drawings, poetry, etc. Today, there is no real concrete movement; the social justice struggles of today are not as easily distinguishable as in past years. For instance, the overt racism of the past has been supplanted by covert racism and discrimination that hides behind policies and politics (Lopez, 2003; Tatum, 2007; Wilson, 2009). Dyson (2007) agrees, "A critical difference between the Black Arts Movement and conscious rap is that hip hop has not been supported by a vibrant political movement. Although many younger figures are politically active, today's artists have a more difficult time identifying with any particular movement, since there has been a severe diminution of social resistance and political rebellion" (p. 66). Once again, educators play a key role in informing their students, raising consciousness levels, and advocating for change. "While black music at its best has often supplied a supplementary argument for political change, it is not a substitute for actual politics. And if you don't have a vital political movement, the music can only go so far" (p. 67). Ultimately, educators need to examine the ways in which they can influence their students to change aspects of hip-hop culture and ways that they can use hip-hop culture to reach out to their students. As one respondent remarked:

> Another strategy would be to integrate hip hop culture as an opportunity for learning. Do you not find it amazing that some of our children can recite word for word lyrics of some songs yet struggle with reading recognition and comprehension? Music can be a mode of learning for some of our children. We need to learn more about hip hop in order to make valuable connections with our students. We do not need to condone negative values such as violence and the objectification of females but it can open up lines of communication. We have to be aware of the power of hip hop.

Recommendations and Implications

The data presented here has important implications for teachers and educational leaders. For teachers in classrooms, this pilot study expands the boundaries of culturally relevant pedagogy and leadership. Hip-hop music and themes can be skillfully and carefully integrated into classrooms to reach students. Although some detractors may disagree with this approach as non-traditional and pandering to students, educators have used hip-hop in education with success (Hill, 2009; Morrell & Duncan-Andrade, 2002). At the same time, it is imperative for educators not to over-rely on these approaches. Hill (2009) reminds educators that "it is important not to romanticize the use of hip-hop texts...the tension between challenging school-sanctioned knowledge and providing students with bodies of knowledge that are requisite for mainstream educational success is one that must be carefully negotiated by hip-hop-based scholars" (p. 124). Thus, we recognize that there are limitations of culturally relevant pedagogy. It is possible for a teacher to connect and have good relationships with their students and still fall short of properly providing a rigorous and challenging educational experience (Beachum et al., 2008). At the same time, teachers should rethink the power relationships between themselves and their students. We are not saying that teachers should give up all classroom authority and power. We are suggesting that teachers not exclusively position themselves as the sole repositories of knowledge and experiences in a classroom (Freire, 2000). If learning is truly a lifelong process, then teachers should remember that as they are teaching, they are also learning. Since hip-hop has proven to have a huge impact on students' lives, educators should make more of an attempt to understand its history and proliferation, clarify its negative aspects for students, and channel its power in positive ways to enhance students' classroom experience.

We have also identified several implications for educational leaders. First, educational leaders should have the wisdom and vision to allow progressive pedagogical approaches, such as the incorporation of hip-hop in classrooms. Too many leaders are reluctant to challenge traditional bodies of knowledge, especially in an era of increased accountability and high-stakes testing. It is essential that educational leaders take seriously their roles as instructional leaders and make room for new approaches and strategies to enhance student learning (Alston, 2002). The essence of leadership requires vision, sacrifice, and the courage to stand by one's convictions and decisions (Cunningham & Cordeiro, 2003; Starratt, 2004; West, 2008). Second, educational leaders should foster a sense of enhanced understanding. This notion is rooted in recognizing the specific variables that create the urban context and its impact on the students. In other words, this means knowing where the students are coming from and not necessarily using this against them. Once again, educational leaders should not give up their roles as disciplinarians; this is a normal and necessary part of their job functions. At the same time, they get a fair amount of latitude in determining how a student will be disciplined. This may mean that a student should not "get the book thrown at them for wearing a hat or 'sagging.'" This may actually be a chance for a caring and knowledgeable administrator (McCray & Beachum, 2006) to start a dialogue with a student as to why they wear their clothes the way that they do and why the school may have a policy against such displays (possibly reducing cultural collision). Similarly, this may also mean that school leaders should update their policies to address things such as sagging pants, texting, cell phones and handheld devices, and coded language (text message shorthand) that is unfamiliar to adults (e.g., lol—laughing out loud; rofl—rolling on the floor laughing; ct—can't talk; cuns—see you in school; dyhag—do you have a girlfriend?; gi—Google it; zzz—sleeping, bored, tired). The reality is that kids are using hip-hop language and/or combinations of text message shorthand to operate in a world that is foreign to many adults. In order for educators to maintain a sense of order in classrooms and schools, they should make a concerted effort to learn the language of our youth (see http://www.netlingo.com/acronyms.php). Educational leaders should be at the forefront of these efforts. Finally, educational leaders should be good role models for students. Unfortunately, many students adopt hip-hop culture's brightest stars as role models because they are unfamiliar with other role models that they may encounter at school (McCray, 2008). Administrators can be more than hard-nosed bureaucrats, managers, and/or disciplinarians. It is important for students to see the human side of administrators and realize that these educators may be more accessible than other role models who may be far away from urban communities. Beachum and McCray (2008) stated it is necessitous for students to "see the leadership in schools actively and actually living the values they espouse in an effort to deter skepticism and accusations of hypocrisy" (p. 113). Educational leaders have the charge to provide progressive educational environments, genuinely care about their students and the communities they come from, and be role models for students who may not have many options.

Conclusion

In this chapter, we have examined hip-hop music and culture, their place in academic literature, and educators' perceptions of their impact and influence on youth. We also discussed these educators' views of hip-hop culture and school culture as well as provided recommendations and implications for classroom teachers and educational leaders. Our final thoughts on this topic are probably best stated by Dyson (2001) who wrote:

> Given its universal popularity and its troubling effects, hip-hop is a vital cultural language that we had all better learn. To ignore its genius, to romanticize its deficits, or to bash it with undiscerning generalities is to risk the opportunity to engage our children about perhaps the most important cultural force in their lives (p. 138).

Chapter Seven

Constructing a Positive Intrasection of Race and Class for the 21st Century

The proper image of our society has never been a melting pot. In bad times, it is a boiling pot; in good times, it is a tossed salad. For those who are in, this is all very well. But the price has always been paid by those who are out, and when they do get in, they do not always get in through a process of mutual accommodation under a broad umbrella of consensus (Theodore Lowi, 1971, p. 53).

On any given Wednesday night, many middle-class and elite middle-class Black Americans can be found in front of our television sets watching Tyler Perry's show, *Meet the Browns*, which some might indicate is the antithesis of the Bill Cosby show back in the 1980s. Our purpose? To clandestinely soak up (i.e., within our own homes) the "authentically" desirable African American culture that many of us failed to attain growing up in our middle-class neighborhoods and schools. A more appropriate terminology for this endeavor would be *technological slumming*.

Alas, the problem arises when both patriarchs—Heathcliff Huxtable, the character from Cosby's show, and Mr. Brown, the character from Perry's show—appear with us in front of our White colleagues and friends. It creates a bit of a quagmire. We had no trouble allowing Mr. Brown to come into our homes via the television set and entertain us with his authentically African American working class mannerisms, but when it comes to acknowledging and embracing those like him outside the Black utopia, this is where the problem arises. The distressing part is that the Mr. Brown character is not even close to the perceived "worst" that lower-wealth African American communities have to offer, the ones who make middle-class Blacks feel so uncomfortable.

Introduction

Today in the 21st century, it seems that America has finally come of age with the issue of race and race relations, at least from the perspective of personal one-on-one interaction. Even though covert institutional racism is still manifested through many media, personal interracial interaction has been diffused to a significant degree (Blum, 2002). African Americans have come a long way from the days of entrenched Jim Crow laws in the Deep South—laws designed to keep African Americans in an inferior position. These edicts dictated where African Americans could dine, which movie theater they could attend, which water fountain and restroom they could use, and of course, in which schools and neighborhoods they could study and reside (Quarles, 1987). These objectionable edicts that were entrenched, not only in many areas in the Deep South, but also in some parts of the North, eroded chances of many African Americans formulating meaningful experiences with Whites on an intellectual, social, political, or economic stage.

However, with the ruling of *Brown v. Board of Education* in 1954, the passage of the Civil Rights Act in 1964, and President Lyndon Johnson's emphatic declaration a year later to take affirmative steps to ensure that all Americans find equality under the law concerning job opportunities, African Americans slowly began to find economic and social parity with middle-class Whites (Cox, 1994; Hu-DeHart, 2001).

As African Americans gained more economic, political, and social rights in the latter part of the 20th century and began to critically evaluate themselves and their conditions, they became more upwardly mobile, navigating different classes while continuing to fight for social justice and equality. "So there [was] a revolutionary change in the Negro's evaluation of his nature and destiny, and a determination to achieve freedom and human dignity" (King, 1958, pp. 13–14). This quotation by Dr. Martin Luther King, Jr. concerning African Americans' plight and conditions rings loud and clear today in the 21st century.

African Americans can be found in every imaginable class in the American class strata, yet they still face overwhelming obstacles as they seek to live a life free from bigotry, prejudice, and racism. Alas, some of the difficulties that African Americans still face, as related to race relations and definitively claiming their place within middle-class American society, are linked to vestiges of the "master identity" (Lacy, 2007). This master identity disproportionately benefits individuals within our society who are "European American, upper-middle class, English speaking, and male" (Nieto, 2000, p. 35). In essence, the master identity construct serves to maximize the cultural and social capital (Loury, 2002) of those who fit the aforementioned societal criteria (Lacy, 2007; Rothenberg, 1998). The leftover rudiments of race relations, from intense segregation to the master identity construct, are not as easily debunked in the 21st century as those who articulate the notion of post-racialism would have us believe. Thus, there needs to be a critical analysis concerning the extent to which the *intrasection* of race and class has impacted African Americans' ability to copiously enjoy what the founding fathers promised in the Declaration of Independence: a God-given right to life, liberty, and the pursuit of happiness.

The term *intrasection* is being used here as it relates to the intersection of race and class within a particular ethnic group: African Americans. In essence, the intrasection of race and class highlights how the race of the African American affects one's class status and, alas, how the issue of class within the African American community permeates racism even further.

This chapter will provide some transparency with regard to how the intrasection of race and class negatively affects African Americans in their effort to fight against class injustice. For example, there has been an explicit historical attempt to definitively connect race and class—that is, Whites generally belong to a more elite class and African Americans generally belong to a lower class stratum. As such, a manufactured perception of race and class is powerfully ingrained within the American psyche, and it has successfully created a quagmire for middle-class Blacks in their effort to fight against class injustice. For many middle-class Blacks, the work of fighting against classism today is limited by a strong intrasection of race and class. This writing attempts to infuse sociological theoretical concepts with strands of critical race theory to provide insight into the potential barriers of middle-class Blacks' amalgamation with African Americans of lower socioeconomic means.

Exclusionary boundary-work (Lacy, 2007) is a principle derived from the field of sociology to explain the effort of individuals to demarcate and differentiate themselves from an otherwise induced and helpless placement within certain class strata of society. This thought is expanded along with the concept of counternarrative and the permanence of racism, both tenets of Critical Race Theory (DeCuir & Dixson, 2004). These concepts will be used to explore the ever-increasing quagmire of the intrasection of race and class that many middle-class Blacks encounter.

Lacy (2007) indicated that many Blacks from middle-class backgrounds participate in exclusionary boundary-work in order to distinguish their status from socioeconomically disadvantaged African Americans as a way to limit the impact of the daily double—that is, the negative impact of racism and classism. Exclusionary boundary-work is the processes where middle-class Blacks engage in a middle-class thought, residence, and aesthetic pattern to deflect the discrimination that comes with the lack of master identity characteristics (Lacy, 2007). Exclusionary boundary-work, along with the permanence of racism (Bell, 1992), is used here to call for a new paradigm—namely, a positive intrasection among middle-class Blacks and African Americans of lower-wealth communities. This new paradigm takes aim at the historical notion of Black solidarity having the ability to bring about such contact, suggesting its replacement with an insurgency model—a model that could adequately serve in bringing about a positive intrasection of race and class among African Americans.

Compelling Context for Positive Intrasectionality of Race and Class among African Americans

The Mark of a Subservient Class

From the moment the first Africans arrived on the shores of Virginia in 1619 (Jordan, 1968; Quarles, 1987), the meaning and construction of race became a major preoccupation with the colonists (Breen & Innes, 1980). As the 17th Century came to a close, it became quite clear that America would become a society where one group would have an ingrained mark as a subservient class (Blassingame, 1979; Breen & Innes, 1980; Jordan, 1968; Quarles, 1987; Stuckey, 1987; Wood, 1974). This mark would exist in the form of skin pigmentation and phenotype, what is known as one's race (Jordan, 1968). Jordan found that "Negroes represented something of an answer to the problem of identification with regards to free labor. Their distinctive appearance was one attribute which might initially have led masters to prefer Negroes as such to white servants" (p. 108).

In the early history of the American colonials, this mark of the subservient class was operationalized through slave codes. Such codes were designed to keep the newly arrived Africans in an acquiescent frame of mind, which provided insurance of their being relegated to a permanent subservient class. Such slave codes ushered African Americans into a "hereditary lifetime service" (Jordan, 1968, p. 73), distinguishing them from their White indentured counterparts. The notion of chattel slavery was also pivotal during this time in undergirding the idea of African Americans as a subservient class. Chattel slavery consisted of African Americans being the real property of a few Whites, thereby making African Americans taxable, inheritable, and of course profitable.

The edicts (i.e., slave codes) in the colonial era that negatively affected African Americans would evolve into more stern laws in the 19th Century, as undergirded by the courts. Such laws would solidify the African American race as a subservient class of people well into the mid-20th century.

Just as court cases on the legal front managed to ensure that African Americans would become a people relegated to an acquiescent state, it took strong progressive court cases such as *Brown v. Board of Education and* a multitude of Civil Rights legislation to debunk the years of racial indoctrination that asserted African Americans were indeed placed on this planet to serve (Feagin, 2001). However, two of the court cases in the 19th century had furthered the propaganda of African Americans as a subservient class: the *Dred Scott* Decision of 1857 and the *Plessy v. Ferguson* case in 1896.

Both of these cases delineated the role of African Americans in the United States. Although the *Dred Scott* Decision, in substance, allowed slavery into the federal territories, the case also had a more insidious aspect to it regarding the rights and status of African Americans in the near future (Quarles, 1987). The *Plessy v. Ferguson* case also served to ensure the role of African Americans as second class beings (albeit, by this time, as second class citizens, with the passage of the Fourteenth Amendment in 1868). This case legally ushered in segregation among African Americans and Whites for more than fifty years, until *Brown v. Board of Education* began the process of dismantling it from a *de jure* perspective; that is, one might view *Brown* as having brought about desegregation but not integration. *De jure* segregation was the process by which segregation was legalized by court cases such as *Plessy v. Ferguson*, whereas *de facto* segregation was a matter of fact, but not legally sanctioned.

With the historical combinations of slave codes, laws, and court decisions designed to keep African Americans in a state of subservience, and many White Americans in the practice of maintaining such a status quo, there was a parallel counter-narrative being presented by progressive Black voices who were articulating a need for Black solidarity to combat the historical pronounced indictment of Blackness as a subservient class. Such voices were with merit, as they attempted to debunk the narrative of Black inferiority and advocate for Black solidarity. According to Loury (2002),

> The arbitrary bodily marks associated with racial distinctions are among the structures in our social environment to which meanings about the identity, capability and worthiness of their bearers have been imputed. . . ."Race" is all

about embodied social signification. In this sense, it is a social truth that race is quite real, despite what may be the biological-taxonomic truth of the claim that there are not races. (p. 58)

Loury proffered how critical it is to acknowledge the role of race in our society; alas, this truth has had a devastating impact on those in the United States who had such arbitrary bodily marks. Thus, Black solidarity has its origins in the fight for racial justice for those who had the mark of the subservient class.

Black Solidarity in the Pre-Brown Era

Before *Brown v. Board of Education* in 1954—the case that made segregation within schools illegal and provided a clear demarcation in American history for gradually ushering in a new attitude concerning race—most African Americans found solace in one another in the form of group solidarity, regardless of class distinction (Shelby, 2005). Even though it did not take too much effort to convince African Americans of all classes of the need for Black solidarity, owing to the conditions of many before 1954, there were many times where issues and conflicts arose concerning which general direction African Americans should proceed politically, socially, and educationally for the good of the race.

Martin Robinson Delany, Marcus Garvey, as well as Frederick Douglass were African Americans who fought for Black rights towards the end of the 19th century and the beginning of the 20th century. All three men found it absolutely necessary that Africans Americans, regardless of their plights in life, forge alliances that would better equip them to deal with the imbedded institutional White supremacy that was in existence after slavery and well into the turn of the 20th century (Shelby, 2005). This was the basic premise of the notion of Black solidarity. Delany, Garvey, and Douglas had different strategies concerning how African Americans should proceed in achieving racial justice, in essence, whether to separate completely from the nation or fight for racial rights from within. Their common view, however, was that the mark of the subservient class was too ingrained and embedded in the minds of Whites to be easily overcome without some form of solidarity on economic, political, and social fronts.

Where the efforts of Delany, Garvey, and Douglas for Black solidarity stopped, other efforts were ushered forward by the intellectual work and endeavors of W.E.B. Du Bois. Du Bois was also someone who unapologetically believed in the concept of Black solidarity. For Du Bois, Black solidarity was needed in order for African Americans to overcome the decades of racial insensitivity and degradation that they had experienced throughout the history of the United States (Shelby, 2005). According to Du Bois, "We believe it [is] the duty of the Americans of Negro decent, as a body to maintain their race identity until this mission of the Negro people is accomplished, and the ideal of human brotherhood has become a practical possibility" (As cited in Shelby, 2005, p. 205). This statement is profound in that it called on a certain group of people with a definitively common trait to disregard any political, economic, or social divisions in their effort to continue to fight against the racial injustice that was preventing them from experiencing social, political, and economic equality, which the entire group desired.

One of the ironies of the legacy of the Jim Crow edicts in America before *Brown v. Board of Education* was that it actually allowed for the Black solidarity that Du Bois spoke of to come to fruition. Before 1954, the majority of African Americans resided in segregated housing patterns in the North as well as in the South; this housing pattern consisted of middle-class Blacks who lived in close proximity with poorer African Americans (Quarles, 1987). With the reality of prosperous African Americans (i.e. doctors, attorneys, educators, ministers, and entrepreneurs) neighboring with African Americans who were economically disadvantaged, there lay the possibility of a concerted effort to fight the anti-Black racism that had had an impact on both groups of African Americans (Shelby, 2005). This particular proximity is something that Du Bois had found useful in his exhortations on Black solidarity, seeing its necessity concerning the alleviation of racism. According to Shelby (2005), Du Bois indeed believed that the proximity of upwardly mobile African Americans with others from lower socioeconomic backgrounds would allow the upwardly mobile Blacks to "make common cause with more disadvantaged [sic] Blacks to resist anti-Black racism and to broaden the scope of opportunity for all Blacks, which would nec-

essarily include addressing the problems of racial inequality and ghetto poverty" (p. 86).

Post-Brown and Black Solidarity

With the landmark ruling of *Brown v. Board of Education*; many subsequent rulings following *Brown* that attempted to dismantle desegregation and Jim Crow laws (e.g., *Green v. County School Board, Swann v.
Charlotte–Mecklenburg Board of Education*, and *Freeman v. Pitts*); along
with civil rights laws (i.e., Title VI and Title VII of the Civil Rights Act
of 1964) and Affirmative Action plans; many Blacks were afforded the
opportunity to move into certain neighborhoods once considered off-
limits and to attend selective schools that historically had not been
viable options. The increasing economic, educational, and social opportunities increasing for many African Americans inevitably led to a larger fissure along class lines within the African American community.
This widening gap thus began to threaten the very strategy that Du Bois
had once advocated for fighting the mark of the subservient class, which
had relegated all African Americans to second-class citizenship.

Lacy (2007) has found that as African Americans achieve higher levels of education and more economic wealth in the post-segregation era,
they begin to move out of traditionally segregated Black neighborhoods
with class heterogeneity and into more racially mixed neighborhoods,
as well as into all Black neighborhoods that reflect their new class status. Lacy pointed out that many middle-class Blacks today can be found
in three distinctive neighborhoods: ones that are racially mixed, some
that are all Black but towards the lower end of the middle-class spectrum, and others that are all-Black elite neighborhoods. Dyson (2005)
opined that the self-separation of middle-class Blacks from African
Americans of lower socio-economic strata had a damaging impact on the
Black solidarity movement for which historic figures such as W. E. B. Du Bois
had long pushed.

Oxymoronic Dent in Black Solidarity

Even with the metamorphosis of Black neighborhoods from a mosaic
community of Black personalities and diverse classes to neighborhoods

based more on wealth and class, the lingering issue that remains for African Americans is the mark of the subservient class. There is still the issue of Blackness, as used since the inception of the United States to distinguish and separate Africans who were brought to America on slave ships from those who came here in search of religious freedom and to escape persecution (Jordan, 1968). However, as stated earlier, the metamorphosis of Black neighborhoods into neighborhoods of class havens for middle-class Blacks has made the notion of Black solidarity increasingly problematic.

Many African Americans who were educated at elite schools and who accumulated capital sought to prove to White society that they were not from an impoverished background—a concept that Lacy (2007) defined as boundary exclusion. Because the notion of Blackness is almost innately ingrained in the minds of many White Americans as being synonymous with a subservient status, as well as a state of poverty (Loury, 2002), a quandary has developed with regards to the historical notion of Black solidarity. Alas, the concept and status of Blackness have carried over from the early settlement of the United States well into the 21st century. Many well-to-do Blacks still find themselves facing discrimination in the job market, social settings, and housing (Lacy, 2007). Middle-class Blacks experience discrimination, and it has in many instances prevented them from excelling at the job. African Americans are often followed in department stores, and frequently experience redlining, where banks refuse to lend money to qualified borrowers. This has forced many Blacks into practicing not only boundary-work, but exclusionary boundary–work, that is, middle-class Blacks will place a geographical distance as well as an identity distance between themselves and African Americans from lower wealth communities, in an attempt to deflect the discrimination that comes with a strong intrasection of race and class (Lacy, 2007). According to Lacy (2007),

> A key component of the public identities asserted by middle-class blacks is based on class and involves differentiating themselves from lower-class blacks through…exclusionary boundary-work.…Middle class blacks are firm that it is possible to minimize the probability of encountering racial discrimination if they can successfully convey their middle-class status to white strangers. To

accomplish this feat,...[middle-class blacks] attempt to erect exclusionary boundaries against a bundle of stereotypes commonly associated with lower class blacks. (p. 75)

Lacy (2007) went on to posit that exclusionary boundary-work by middle-class Blacks comes in many different forms, from dressing exceedingly well when entering a department store and riding with a realtor, to displaying an attitude disposition in the work place—what Lacy called *script switching*. However, script switching is somewhat different from the readily known term, *code switching*, where individuals modify language in order to make transparent their middle-class status. Lacy explained that script switching involves middle-class Blacks employing concerted strategies "to demonstrate that they are knowledgeable about middle-class lifestyles and to communicate their social positions to others" (p. 88). Thus, their effort of social identity construction to set a clear demarcation between themselves and the poorer African Americans becomes *social differentiation*, where middle-class Blacks try to make it as clear as possible to others that they are different from poorer African Americans. Exclusionary boundary-work occurs not only when African Americans are interacting with Whites, but also when African Americans are interacting with other African Americans:

> Like most people,...[middle-class blacks] prefer to interact with others much like themselves, blacks who share their values and lifestyles. Thus, the black community that parents are at pains to expose their children to—the world that adults look forward to reconnecting with at the end of the day—is one carefully bounded by class. Defining themselves in class terms through their interaction with likeminded people allows middle-class blacks to signal their exclusive place in the black class structure and to regulate which individuals gain entry to the black middle-class. (p. 173)

What Lacy has described occurs because of the permanence of racism and the stigma that racial category carries with it (Loury, 2002). The withdrawal of middle-class Blacks into their safe havens of residential patterns allows them to deflect some of the obstacles that racial stigma may bring upon them. According to Loury (2002),

> Because race conventions can seem to be natural and quite consistent with reason, and because they convey significant social meanings, people with partic-

ular race-markers may become stigmatized—seen by their fellows as "dam-aged[sic] goods," as THEM not US, as persons [who] lack the ability or "cul-ture" to succeed in society's mainstream. (p. 111)

Because of the permanence of racism (Bell, 1992) along with the racial stigma that has been ingrained into the American psyche—that is, the image of Blackness being relegated to poverty and servitude—it has cre-ated an oxymoronic fissure between middle-class Blacks and African Americans from lower social economic backgrounds. This has in essence eliminated any altruistic racial solidarity that the likes of Delaney, Garvey, Douglas, and Du Bois once spoke of in support of Black libera-tion.

Moving from Black Solidarity to an Insurgency Model

The notion of Black solidarity has been defined, redefined, and modified over time to embody the needs of Black America during turbulent times of fighting for racial equality and equity. But because racial conflict is no longer readily observable or overt as in years past (Lopez, 2003; Loury, 2002), the notion of Black solidarity to fight racism seems antiquated and outdated to many, especially in the era of the work of boundary exclu-sion. Many scholars from a variety of fields (Bell, 1992; DeCuir & Dixson, 2004; Dyson, 2003; Feagin, 2001; Lacy, 2007; Shelby, 2005; West, 1993) have devoted a considerable amount of time on the issue of race and posit that racism can still be found throughout the fabric of America. Lopez (2003) added that because racism has historically been linked to overt representation of oppression—including lynching, Jim Crow laws, and hurtful rhetoric—many feel that racism in America has been total-ly eradicated.

As stated earlier, in an oxymoronic way, the permanence of racism along with the mark of the subservient class has potentially led to the failure of Black solidarity in the fight against racial injustice. It is because of the permanence of racism and racial stigmatization (Loury, 2002) that a fault line between middle-class Blacks and African Americans of lower wealth has come into existence. Thus, the work of boundary exclusion has in many instances resulted in a limited amount of positive intrasection between race and class for many middle-class Blacks (Dyson, 2005; Lacy, 2007; Shelby, 2005).

With this faltering positive intrasectionality between middle-class Blacks and poorer African Americans and the waning notion of Black solidarity, a new model is needed in order to allow African Americans from different classes to form a positive intrasectionality on the lines of race and class. Insurgency is definitely a time-tested panacea in the fight for social justice. Many groups in societies across the world, as well as in the United States, have used the insurgency model in order to secure economic and political rights. The farm worker movement in the United States used such a model in the 1960s in order to secure political and economic rights (Jenkins, 1985); the working-class women of France carried out a political insurgency to secure their rights in the mid-19th century (Barry, 1996); and African Americans along with women, students, and auto workers used the insurgency model in the 1960s to force America to begin to live up to its founding principles (Geschwender, 1977; Jenkins, 1985). The insurgency model would be somewhat new to African Americans of today. During the 1960s, when the insurgency model was used as part of the Civil Rights Movement, African Americans, in order to secure political and economic enfranchisement, aligned themselves with influential progressive Whites who were in positions of authority throughout society (Jenkins, 1985). The vast discontent of African Americans with the laws and policies of the United States during this time was displayed through civil disobedience as well as militant insurrections. Such activities caught the attention of many liberal Whites and awakened their social justice conscience. This conscience-awakening among broadminded Whites allowed for the mobilization of additional resources to help African Americans begin to secure economic and political equality (Jenkins, 1985).

Even though Dr. Martin Luther King, Jr., along with other African American leaders and progressive Whites, tried to ensure that African Americans would sit at the table of economic and political prosperity; many poor African Americans in urban and rural areas today have not yet obtained a seat at such a table. President Barack Obama had acknowledged this at one of his election campaign rallies when he spoke of the many individuals in urban cities who are engaging in daily "quiet riots" of despair and hopelessness, hoping that someone is listening to their struggles.

So, what makes the insurgency model different from the group solidarity model that was practiced by African Americans throughout U.S. history to secure enfranchisement within American society? Part of the answer entails the aforementioned statement by President Obama concerning whether someone is listening to the cries of Blacks of low socioeconomic means. Amid the struggles of African Americans for racial justice, from slavery to the Civil Rights Movement of the 1960s, the common denominator of those involved was that they all had the mark of the subservient class and, in the eyes of most Whites, were in the same class stratum regardless of their economic and educational attainment. The insurgency was carried out only when liberal and progressive Whites with resources immersed themselves into the struggles in order to help change "structural powers" (Jenkins, 1985, p. 20). In essence, the Civil Rights Movement produced an insurgency (a movement with the involvement of liberal and progressive Whites) as well as a continuation of Black solidarity (a movement where Blacks coalesced to fight for racial justice).

Jenkins (1985) proffered that an effective insurgency allows previously disenfranchised groups to become part of economic and political power in a demarcated and measurable way: "Political elites sponsor the entry of the more powerful insurgencies and institutionalized social reform that, in part, address their demands" (p. 27). This statement is profound and almost contradictory in the sense that most insurgencies are successful when the insurgents are almost exclusive in group membership. In many cases where antagonists join subordinates in the insurrection for economic and political power, there is a fear among the subordinates with regard to trust and paternalistic control (Jenkins, 1985). However, without such support of those with political and economic power, the gains among the insurgents are marginal at best.

With middle-class African Americans having more access to political and economic power today than at any point in American history, a climate for an insurgency is created, as undergirded by the positive intrasectionality of race and class. Today the notion of Black solidarity is almost passé. However, an insurgency that connects race and class is needed today, probably more than at any other point in history. Today, there does not seem to be any cognitive dissonance in the American psyche about the ill-fated plight of poor African Americans in many urban and rural areas of society (Loury, 2002). Similarly, there does not appear to be any dissonance in the American consciousness with regard to the 1 million-plus African American men who are incarcerated (Loury, 2002). Now, in the 21st century, there is no apparent dissonance in the American psyche with regard to the thousands of students who attend school hungry on a daily basis (Kozol, 1991). And there does not seem to be any conflict in the American psyche concerning the high crime rate in many urban areas among the poor. Further, there appears to be no cognitive dissonance with regard to the high dropout rate among urban students and the lack of financial resources, which makes their schools ill-equipped for high achieving (Kozol, 1991). Cognitive dissonance does not exist as it relates to the conditions of many African Americans due to the fact that the plight and status of most African Americans is aligned with the notion of the mark of the subservient class, which is entrenched in the American psyche. Loury (2002) insisted that

> What is required, instead is a commitment on the part of the public, the political elite, the opinion-shaping media, and so on to take responsibility for such situations as the contemporary plight of the urban black poor, and to understand them in a general way as a conquest of an ethically indefensible past. (p. 127)

Thus, the functionality of middle-class Blacks in an insurgency role, fighting for increased social justice, is to use their political and economic influence to shape media opinion as well as policy with regard to African Americans of lower socio-economic means; and to immerse themselves in paradoxical boundary inclusion work. Lacy (2007) explained that boundary inclusion involves middle-class Blacks' use of script switching to avoid potential discrimination. According to Lacy (2007), "[some] middle-class blacks feel compelled to draw inclusionary boundaries, that is, they employ public identities to erase the distinctions between their group and the white middle-class" (p. 225). Lacy went on to state how it is certainly understandable why middle-class Blacks, in accordance with other groups, even middle-class Whites, might want to embark on the role of impression management. However, the conjoined boundary-work of inclusion and exclusion among middle-class Blacks potentially drives them away further from poorer African Americans. As such, it damages their humanity concerning positive intrasectionality of race and class, and it proves to be an oxymoronic disservice to legitimating their own status in society. Regardless of how much boundary-work is produced by middle-class Blacks and Black elites, the notion of the subservient class is still ingrained in the psyche of many White Americans.

This notion of a subservient class will not ultimately decrease until poverty in inner cities has dissipated, the incarceration rate among African American men has dramatically gone down, and poorer African Americans are empowered by educational opportunities. As Shelby (2005) articulated in the spirit of W.E.B. Du Bois, "[middle-class blacks] can make common cause with more disadvantage[d] blacks to resist anti-black racism and to broaden the scope of opportunity for all blacks, which would necessarily include addressing the racial inequality and ghetto poverty" (p. 86). Finally, the field of education is one area in which the paradoxical work of boundary inclusion is needed between middle-class Blacks and poorer African Americans.

Insurgency for Educational Empowerment

While visiting a friend of mine who lives in another major urban area, I had the distinct pleasure of venturing out to an urban middle school to participate in a program where judges and lawyers went into a school once a week to read to students. The purpose of the program is two-fold. First, it is designed to have the young boys and girls at the school become more interested in reading. Each Friday, the students select a book to read and discuss with the attorneys and judges the following week. The second aspect of the reading program is to have the students become inspired by seeing individuals of renowned esteem come into the school. This adventure is the kind of effort I am referring to concerning the boundary-work of paradoxical inclusion, where middle-class and elite Blacks do the work of breaking down boundaries that have separated them from poorer African Americans.

Unfortunately, the verdict for many of our schools in urban areas that educate and prepare students of color for our global economy is fair at best, and in dire straits at worst. The reading program in this major city is a microcosm of programs across the nation where middle-class and elite African Americans go into urban schools to try to make a difference. This positive intrasectionality of class and race is drastically needed in the educational arena. Gordon (2006) has found that the state of many schools that educate Black children is more along the continuum of dire straits. Gordon emphasized that 50 years after the *Brown* decision—a decision that was supposed to bring about integration into schools— African American students attend schools that are predominately Black and vice versa for White students. Gordon went on to point out that "by almost all the common indicators of academic achievement and school quality, students who identify themselves as black suffer in comparison with students who identify themselves as white" (p. 26). Noguera (2003) also found that "Urban schools and the children who attend them languish under third world-like conditions . . ." (p. 14).

The issues that Gordon (2006) and Noguera (2003) illuminate as they critique the plight of Black education center on systemic structural problems. Such issues consist of the continued segregation of schools where students of color attend schools that are *de facto* segregated. Other issues include the level of funding received by predominately minority schools in urban and rural areas, as well as the quality of teaching within these schools. Beachum et al. (2008) have found that

> the low quality of teaching, the lack of teacher information of and access to new or relevant pedagogical methods suggests [sic] the lack of rights of teachers of African American students to gain new skills and to develop stronger teaching methods....Students of color, then, living in mostly segregated...settings...do not receive the same rights of access and enjoyment of curriculum and quality teaching awarded to whites students, who live and attend schools in mostly suburban, more affluent settings. (p. 203)

The aforementioned systemic structural problems that many Black students from lower socioeconomic backgrounds experience are indicative of a continued cycle of poverty that exists among Blacks of lower socioeconomic backgrounds.

Thus, the boundary-work of paradoxical inclusion where middle-class Blacks and Black elites form insurgencies with poorer African Americans to break the cycle of poverty must be communal in its structure. Paradoxical inclusion and insurgency that bring about a communal effort of positive intrasectionality of race and class can have an impact on class inequities. The abatement of such class inequities could lead to a collapse of the mark of the subservient class, but the work must begin with community uplift for all (Beachum, Obiakor, & McCray, 2007). The concept of community uplift theory (Beachum et al., 2007) calls on all African Americans of different classes to work together for the betterment of the African American community as a whole. Beachum et al. (2007) posited that community uplift theory is a comprehensive philosophy for the effective change to a more Afrocentric value system.

Community uplift theory is derived from the seven principles of Nguzo Saba (Karenga, 1989) that emphasize individual and collective efforts among Blacks. The individual efforts stress such values as determination, purpose, and creativity; whereas the collective efforts accentuate principles such as unity, collective work and responsibility, and cooperative economics. Various scholars believe that individual values, along with the collective principles highlighted by Karenga (1989), are needed for improvement of the education that many black youth are now experiencing (Alford, McKeny, & Gavazzi, 2001; Beachum et. al., 2007; Dyson, 1997; Karenga, 1989; Perry, Steele, & Hilliard, 2003; Shelby, 2005). The collective principle requires middle-class Blacks and Black elites to engage the poorer Black communities in the area of cooperative economics and collective work and responsibility. Not only are collective values called upon to enhance insurgent efforts to improve the plight of African-Americans in lower socioeconomic communities, but such principles are part of what is needed in a new and revamped curriculum that could ensure a long-term insurgency among middle-class Blacks and poorer Blacks.

Blacks in the inner cities and impoverished rural areas who make it to the Black middle class will undoubtedly espouse individual values of determination, purpose, and creativity. However, in order to foster such an insurgency between middle-class Blacks and poorer African

Americans, a curriculum must be present in these schools to ensure that a positive intrasectionality of race and class is part of the psyche of such individuals who escape poverty.

Efforts need to start with a curriculum of empowerment to ensure that African-Americans practice paradoxical boundary inclusion when they are fortunate to make it out of the slums and into middle-class society. Such empowerment for African American students include going beyond the limited and poorly funded No Child Left Behind Act (Hunter & Bartee, 2003; Karp, 2002; Noguera, 2004). This act has oxymoronically generated inertia in many schools with regard to the educative experience of poorer students. It called for excellence in poorer schools by ensuring rigorous standards in the areas of language arts, mathematics, and science (Hoy & Miskel, 2005), while asking for the disaggregated data analysis of specific student sub-groups (i.e., economically poor students with limited English-speaking ability, and students of color) (Cunningham & Cordeiro, 2006). With such lofty objectives of excellence, the challenge of many schools has become how to educate students beyond the mandates that are called for in the restricted No Child Left Behind Act.

For those who are fortunate to do well academically, go on to college, and move out of the community, a sense of community empowerment has likely not been instilled. Many Africans Americans who are fortunate to make it out of the slums may hold that they did so by pulling themselves up by their bootstraps and embracing the concept of meritocracy. In essence, some middle-class Blacks might appeal more to the individual values espoused by Karenga (1989)—determination, purpose, and creativity—without acknowledging the principles of unity, collective work and responsibility, and cooperative economics. And such lack of acknowledgement creates even more division between middle-class Blacks and African Americans of lower socioeconomic means. Shelby (2005) opined,

> It is unfair and callous for black elites to preach to those in dark ghettoes about how they ought to conduct their lives when we know that there are not enough jobs, that the public school system [is] in need of radical reform, and that racial discrimination remains a serious problem. We also know that living in severely impoverished conditions shapes the attitudes of the poor toward work and

education. Hence, the poor often fail to develop the skills, credentials, and discipline needed to fare well in a capitalist economy. (p. 145)

Here Shelby clearly demarcates the difference between the preaching rhetoric of "Why can't you do as I do" and an insurgency of positive intrasectionality between middle-class Blacks and poorer African Americans where the collective principles of unity, collective work and responsibility, and cooperative economics are practiced in earnest.

Conclusion

For a severe blow to be directed towards the notion of Blackness as a subservient class, there has to be a drastic eradication in the number of Black men who are incarcerated, as well as the number African American students who drop out of school in many of our urban areas. We believe that these eradications can begin via the positive intrasectionality between middle-class African Americans and African Americans from low wealth communities. For Dr. Martin Luther King, Jr. did admonish us with his ideas in "A Letter from a Birmingham Jail" that "we are caught up in an inescapable network of mutuality, tied in a single garment of destiny. Whatever affects one directly affects all indirectly." And according to Du Bois, such an insurgency is justified if the mission has not been accomplished. As long as a plethora of problems still face Black Americans, alas, the mission is not complete.

Note

This chapter is a reprint from:
McCray, C. R. (2008). Constructing a positive intrasection of race and class for the 21st Century. Journal of School Leadership, 18(2), 249–267.

Afterword

In Honor of the Hip-Hop Culture
Beyond the "Blame Game"

In *Cultural Collision and Collusion: Reflections on Hip-Hop Culture, Values, and Schools*, Beachum and McCray challenge us to think and do. The "thinking" and the "doing" are not mutually inclusive entities since the latter involves more contentious actions. I was reminded of Socrates who sought to shift the paradigms and powers of his time by challenging the Athenian youth to question the arrogance, power, and dominance of the Sophists. Is it any surprise that the Socratic method of instruction is popular in many instructional circles today? As it appears, Beachum and McCray are uninterested in maintaining the status quo that harps on the "blame game" by asking disfranchised people to pull themselves up by their own bootstraps (Obiakor, 2008, 2009). However, they seem interested in thinking "outside the box" to further the understanding that not everyone has boots and that those who have boots might not have straps, and vice versa. Additionally, Beachum and McCray direct their discourse on solution-oriented strategies to remedy the endemic problems confronting urban children and youth, the major make-up of the hip-hop generation.

I have always wondered why today's blame-game toward the hip-hop generation has been at a startling fillip. The shameless frequency of the blame game seems to have some socio-historical or racial underpinnings. For example, there is a logical surmise that "if I do not like someone, I will not like whatever he/she does or whatever is connected to him/her." For many culturally, linguistically, socio-economically, and racially different students, the perception that they are inferior is a daily occurrence. At least, the media presents it that way! These students are viewed as *culturally deprived, linguistically deficient, socio-economically draining, racially inferior*, and even *intellectually deficient*. Some of these belief systems are based on *biological determinism* which tends to exaggerate the myth of socioeconomic dissonance (Gould, 1981; Obiakor, 2001, 2007, 2008, 2009). To a large measure, an underlying racist presumption is that "nothing good can come from these people!" Yet, through these so called people who are the hub of the hip-hop generation, fashion has evolved, music has changed, sports have progressed, our ways of life have changed, money has been made, and our nations and world have advanced culturally. Clearly, in this book, the values espoused by the hip-hop generation are endorsed as positive phenomena in our culture, society, and world.

The Voice of Change

In *Cultural Collision and Collusion*, Beachum and McCray provide the voice of change as they challenge the retrogressive myths about hip-hop culture and values. To a great extent, they recommend what schools, families, communities, and policy makers can do to advance innovative programming for our youth. They reintroduce the "cool pose theory" and discuss "thug theology" as theories that reaffirm self-confidence and self-empowerment of our youth—they do not see these theories as iconoclastic attempts to destabilize our society. In their words, "a more rigorous analysis and critical appreciation of youth is necessary because their issues are complex, multifaceted, and delve deeper than what we might see on television or hear in trite superficial conversation." They conclude that this book provides "a forum for different (and sometimes divergent) methodologies, philosophies, and ideologies." I agree with their conclusion.

Cultural Collision and Collusion, as a book, highlights some of the tensions that develop when the values of our youth collide with the values of our schools. Specifically, it examines the nature of today's schooling and reiterates what pre-service teachers, classroom teachers, and administrators should do to reduce or eliminate cultural collision. It presents challenges and ramifications of cultural collision, especially on young at-risk African American males. In addition, it discusses the *cool pose* and its impact on educational experiences of students. Intertwined with these discussions are the hip-hop behavioral patterns that impinge upon learning and teaching in schools. I agree with the overall premise of this book. The question then becomes, How can we change and grow as we interact with ourselves and others linguistically, socio-economically, and racially different from us? For me, there is a reason and season for us to do well (i.e., valuing fellow human-beings). I believe "we all have the potential to change, but we must challenge ourselves and others for such a change to occur" (Obiakor, 2008, p. iii). Earlier, Chittister (1999) wrote:

> The thought of constant change colors our sense of the future. We wear it like a logo as we race from place to place, and now in our time, from idea to idea, from concept to concept, from social revolution to social revolution…change, after all, is not a given. Change follows in the wake of something that preceded it, quiet as a shift in the wind. It does not just happen; it is not a timed process. "If we're just patient; if we can just wait long enough, it has to come," we say when we do not want to be responsible ourselves for the change. But change does not just come; change is brought somehow. (p. 53)

Prescriptions for Educational Change

In the end, *Cultural Collision and Collusion* prescribes new thinking and new action on how we identify, assess, label, categorize, place, and instruct at-risk urban students. This new thinking and new action have the potential to reduce (a) disproportionate representations of culturally and linguistically diverse (CLD) urban learners in special education programs (Obiakor, 2007, 2008); (b) the Hobson's choice, the "no-choice" choice (i.e., the "take-it-or-leave it" choice) that faces our children and youth with problem behaviors and (c) achievement gaps of many disenfranchised learners in today's changing world (Obiakor, 2009). It is disastrous for our nation's schools to have predominantly CLD learners in programs for students with emotional behavior disorders; and it is equally devastating to have few of these learners in programs for students with gifts and talents. Interestingly, the hip-hop culture has been a creative phenomenon that has totally changed our ways of life! We cannot afford to underplay its positive impacts on our socio-economic well-being. Clearly, it should concern us that our schools are lagging behind in embracing, channeling, and utilizing this phenomenal culture. As Marable (1993) pointed out:

> Our challenge is to revive the idea of education, by forging to conditions in our school systems and national educational policies, to advance the promise of new levels of excellence. Unless we accomplish this, our country lurches toward an inevitable crisis between the affluent, educated "haves" and the undereducated, severely alienated "have nots." The choice is ours, and the time is short. (p. 5A)

Marble's (1993) push for change continues to be relevant today. Teachers, service providers, and administrators cannot expect miracles to happen in their educational programs without their positive efforts to engage members of the hip-hop generation. These professionals are expected to be change-agents and not laggards. In addition, they must create the miracles and sometimes become the miracles that they want to happen (Obiakor, 2008). To a large measure, teachers and service providers must discontinue the "get rid of" students mentality. More than 20 years ago, DeBruyn (1984) warned that:

> If we adopt a "get rid of" attitude, we violate a basic tenet of education: that each student is an individual, and that our instruction and curriculum must try to make allowances for individual differences. Regardless of feelings, we cannot discount this tenet. That's why it's dangerous to adopt a practice that amount to saying "get the uninterested, unmotivated, and ill-behaved out of the school to keep those from interfering with those who want to learn." In truth, this is an easy way out. And teaching all students is not easy. Yet, it remains our challenge. (p. 1)

Conclusion

Hip-hop culture and values are now incorporated into our daily lives. Whether we like it or not, that is our reality today! Beachum and McCray's *Cultural Collision and Collusion* brings this reality to life. They challenge educators, service providers, and administrators to go beyond the blame game to work with at-risk or disenfranchised urban learners, a fundamental group of the hip-hop generation. As a result, we must value these learners and provide them with opportunities and choices for growth in our multicultural world. If and when there are achievement gaps, we must work collaboratively and consultatively to narrow and eliminate them. Finally, to maximize the potential of these learners and to help them survive the trials and tribulations of the hip-hop culture, we must shift our paradigms by knowing who we are; learning the facts when we are in doubt; changing our thinking; using resource persons; building our self-concepts; using divergent techniques; making the right choices; and continuing to learn.

Festus E. Obiakor

References

Adams, M. (2000). Classism. In M. Adams, W. J. Blimenfeld, R. Castaneda, H. W. Hackman, M. L . Peters, X, Zuniga (Eds.), *Readings for diversity and social justice: An anthology on racism, antisemitism, sexism, heterosexism, ableism, and classism.* New York: Routledge.

Akbar, N. (1984). *Chains and images of psychological slavery.* Jersey City, NJ: New Mind Productions.

Alexander, K. L., Entwisle, D. R. (2001). The dropout process in life course perspective: Early risk factors at home and school. *Teacher College Record, 103*(5), 760–822.

Alford, K., McKenry, P., & Gavazzi, S. (2001). Enhancing the achievement in adolescent black males: The rites of passage link. In Richard Majors (Eds.), *Educating our black children: New directions and radical approaches.* New York: Routledge.

Alston, J. A. (2002). *Multi-leadership in urban schools: Shifting paradigms for administration and supervision in the new millennium.* Landham, MD: University Press of America.

Anderson, E. (1999). *Code of the streets: Decency, violence, and the moral life of the inner poor.* Cambridge, MA: Harvard University Press.

Au, W. (2005). Fresh out of school: Rap music's discursive battle with education. *Journal of Negro Education, 74*(3), 210–220.

Ayers, W. (1994). Can city schools be saved? *Educational Leadership, 51*(8), 60–63.

Banks, J. A. (1995). Multicultural education: development, dimensions, and challenges. In J. Joll, (Ed.), *Taking sides: Clashing views on controversial education issues* (pp. 84–93). New York: The Dushkin Publishing Group, Inc.

Banks, J. A. (2001). Multicultural education: Characteristics and goals. In J. A. Banks & C. A. McGee Banks (Eds.), *Multicultural education: Issues and perspectives* (4th ed.), (pp. 3–30). New York: John Wiley & Sons, Inc.

Barry, D. (1996). *Women and political insurgency.* New York: St. Martins Press, Inc.

Beachum, F. D., Dentith, A. M., & McCray, C. R. (2004). Administrators' and teachers' work in a new age of reform: Understanding the factors in African American student success. *E-Journal of Teaching and Learning in Diverse Settings, 2*(1). Available: http://www.subr.edu/coeducation/ejournal/EJTLDS.%20Volume%202%20Issue%201.Beachum%20et%20al.pdf

Beachum, F. D., Dentith, A., & McCray, C. R., & Boyle, T. (2008). Havens of hope or the killing fields: The paradox of leadership, pedagogy, and relationships in an urban middle school. *Urban Education, 43*(2), 189–215.

Beachum, F. D., & McCray, C. R. (2004). Cultural collision in urban schools. *Current Issues in Education, 7*(5). Available: http://cie.asu.edu/volume7/number5/

Beachum, F. D., & McCray, C. R. (2005). Changes and transformations in the philosophy of character education in the 20th Century. *Essays in Education, 14.* Available: http://www.usca.edu/essays/vol142005/beachum.pdf

Beachum F. D., & McCray, C. R. (2008a). Dealing with cultural collision in urban schools: What pre-service educators should know. In G. S. Goodman (Ed). *Education psychology: An application of critical constructivism.* New York: Peter Lang.

Beachum F. D., & McCray, C. R. (2008b). Leadership in the eye of the storm: Challenges at the intersection of urban schools and cultural collusion. *Multicultural Learning and Teaching, 3*(2), 99–120.

Beachum, F. D., & Obiakor, F. E. (2005). Educational leadership in urban schools. In F. E. Obiakor & F. D. Beachum (Eds.), *Urban education for the 21st century: Research, issues, and perspectives* (pp. 83–99). Springfield, IL: Charles C. Thomas.

Beachum, F. D., Obiakor, F. E., & McCray, C. R. (2007). Community uplift theory for positive change of African Americans in urban schools. In M. C. Brown & R. D. Bartee (Eds.), *Still not equal: Expanding educational opportunities in society.* New York: Peter Lang.

Bell, D. (1992). *Faces at the bottom of the well: The permanence of racism.* New York: Basic Books.

Berelson, B., & Steiner, G. A. (1964). *Human behavior: An inventory of scientific findings.* New York: Harcourt, Brace & World.

Berman, S., & Berreth, D. (1997). The moral dimensions of schools. *Educational Leadership, 54*(8), 24–27.

Bissell, W. C. (2005). Engaging colonial nostalgia. *Cultural Anthropology, 20*(2), 215–248.

Black, S. (2004). Beyond zero tolerance. *American School Board Journal, 191*(9), 62–64.

Blanchett, W., Mumford, V., & Beachum, F. D., (2005). Urban school failure and disproportionality in a Post-*Brown* era: Benign neglect of the Constitutional rights of students of color. *Remedial and Special Education, 26*(2), 70–81.

Blassingame, J. W. (1979). *The slave community: Plantation life in the Antebellum South.* New York: Oxford University Press.

Blum, L. (2002). *"I'm not a racist, but...": The moral quandary of race.* Ithaca, NY: Cornell University Press.

Bogotch, I., Beachum, F. D., Blount, J., Brooks, J., & English, F. (2008). *Radicalizing educational leadership: Dimensions of social justice.* Rotterdam, Netherlands: Sense Publishing.

Bowles, S., & Gintis, H. (1976). *Schooling in capitalist America.* London: Routledge and Kegan Paul.

Breen, T. H., & Innes, S. (1980). *Myne owne ground: Race @ freedom on Virginia' Eastern Shores, 1640–1676.* New York: Oxford University Press.

Browder, A. (1989). *From the Browder file: 22 essays of the African American experience.* Washington, DC: The Institute of Karmic Guidance.

Brown, J. D., L'Engle, K. L., Pardun, C. J., Guo, G., Kenneavy, K., & Jackson, C. (2006). Sexy media matter: Exposure to sexual content in music, movies, television and magazines predicts Black and White adolescents' sexual beahavior. *Pediatrics, 117,* 1018–1027.

Bush, L. (1999). *Can Black mothers raise our sons?* Chicago: African American Images.

Cartledge, G., Tillman, L ., & Johnson, C. T. (2001). Professional ethics within the context of student discipline and diversity. *Teacher Education and Special Education, 24*(1), 25–37.

Casella, R. (2003). Zero Tolerance policy in schools: Rationale, consequences, and alternatives. *Teachers College Record, 105*(5), 872–892.

Cassidy, E. F., & Stevenson, H. C. (2005). They wear the mask: Hypervulnerability and hypermasculine aggression among African American males in an urban remedial disciplinary school. *Journal of Aggression, Maltreatment & Trauma, 11*(4), 53–74.

Chaddha, A., Wilson, W. J., & Venkatesh, S. (Summer 2008). In defense of the 'Wire.' *Dissent,* 83–86.

Chideya, F. (1995). *Don't believe the hype: Fighting cultural misinformation about African-Americans.* New York: Penguin Books.

Children's Defense Fund (2003, Feb. 1). Facts on Black youth violence and crime. Retrieved from http://www.childrensdefense.org/ss_ydfs_viocrime_bl.php

Chittister, J. (1999). *There is a season* (3rd printing). Maryknoll, NY: Orbis Books.

Clark, K. B. (1965). *Dark ghetto: Dilemmas of social power.* New York: Harper & Row.

Clay, A. (2003). Keepin' it real: Black youth hip-hop culture, and Black identity. *American Behavioral Scientist, 46*(10), 1346–1358.

Collins, P. H. (2005). *Black sexual politics: African Americans, gender, and the new racism.* New York: Routledge.

Cosby, B., & Poussaint, A. F. (2007). *Come on people: On the path from victims to victors.* Nashville: Thomas Nelson.

Cox, T. H. (1994). *Cultural diversity in organizations: Theory research and practice.* San Francisco: Berrett-Koehler Publishers.

Cox, T., Jr. (2001). *Creating the multicultural organization: A strategy for capturing the power of diversity.* San Francisco: Jossey-Bass.

Creswell, J. (2007). *Qualitative inquiry & research design: Choosing among five approaches.* (2nd ed.). Thousand Oaks, CA: SAGE.

Cunningham, W. G., & Cordeiro, P. A. (2003). *Educational leadership: A problem-based approach* (2nd ed.). Boston: Allyn and Bacon.

Cunningham, W. G., & Cordeiro, P. A. (2006). *Educational leadership: A problem-based approach* (3rd ed.). Boston: Allyn and Bacon.

Cusic, D. (2001). The popular culture economy. *Journal of Popular Culture, 35*(3), 1 10.

Damen, L. (1987). *Culture learning: The fifth dimension on the language classroom.* Reading, MA: Addison-Wesley.

Dantley, M. (2002). Uprooting and replacing positivism, the melting pot, multicultural-ism, and other impotent notions in educational leadership through an African American perspective. *Education and Urban Society, 34*(3), 334–352.

Dantley, M. (2005). African American spirituality and Cornel West's notions of prophet-ic pragmatism: Restructuring educational leadership in American urban schools. *Educational Administration Quarterly, 41*(4), 651–674.

Darder, A., Baltodano, M., & Torres, R. D. (2003). Critical pedagogy: An introduction. In A. Darder, M. Baltodano, & R. D. Torres (Eds.). *The critical pedagogy reader* (pp. 1–21). New York: Routledge.

Davis, K. C., Farrelly, M. C., Messeri, P., & Duke, J. (2009). The impact of national pre-vention campaigns on tobacco-related beliefs. Intentions to smoke and smoke ini-tiation: Results from a longitudinal survey of youth in the United States. *International Journal of Environmental Research and Public Health, 6*(2), 722–740.

Day-Vines, N. L., Day-Hairston, B. O. (2005). Culturally congruent strategies for address-ing the behavioral needs of urban, African American male adolescents. *Professional School Counseling, 8*(1), 236–243.

Deal, T. E., & Peterson, K. D. (1999). *Shaping school culture: The heart of leadership.* San Francisco: Jossey-Bass.

DeBruyn, R. L. (1984, April 16). Upholding the tenets of education. *The Master Teacher, 15*(32),

DeCuir, J. T., & Dixson, A. D. (2004). 'So when it comes out, they aren't that surprise that it is there': Using critical race theory as a tool of analysis of race and racism in edu-cation. *Educational Researcher, 33*(5), 26–31.

Decuir-Gunby, J. T. (2009). A review of racial identity Development of African American adolescents: The role of education. *Review of Educational Research, 79*(1), 103–124.

Delpit, L. (1995). *Other people's children.* New York: New Press.

Dember, W. (1961). *Psychology of perception.* New York: Holt, Rinehart & Winston.

Douglass, F. (1968). *The narrative of the life of Fredrick Douglass: An American slave.* New York: Signet.

Duncan-Andrade, J. (2008). Your best friend or worst enemy: Youth popular culture, pedagogy, and curriculum in urban classrooms. In G. Goodman (Ed.), *Educational psychology: An application of critical constructivism* (pp. 113–143). New York: Peter Lang.

Dyson, M. E. (1996). *Between God and gangsta rap: Bearing witness to black culture.* New York: Oxford University Press.

Dyson, M. E. (1997). *Race rules: Navigating the color line.* New York: Vintage Books.

Dyson, M. E. (2001). *Holler if you hear me: Searching for Tupac Shakur.* New York: Basic Books.

Dyson, M. E. (2003). *Open Mike: Reflections on philosophy, race, sex, culture, and religion.* New York: Basic Civitas Books.

Dyson, M. E. (2004). *The Michael Eric Dyson reader.* New York: Basic Civitas Books.

Dyson, M. E. (2005). *Is Bill Cosby right? Or has the Black middle class lost its mind?* New York: Basic Civitas Books.

Dyson, M. E. (2006). *Come hell or high water: Hurricane Katrina and the color of disaster.* New York: Basic Civitas Books.

Dyson, M. E. (2007). *Know what I mean?: Reflections on hip hop.* New York: Basic Civitas Books.

English, F. W. (2004). Undoing the "done deal": Reductionism, ahistory, and pseudo-science in the knowledge base and standards for educational administration. *UCEA Review, 46*(2), 5–7.

Epps, E. G. (2005). Urban education: Future perspectives. In F. E. Obiakor & F. D. Beachum (Eds.), *Urban education for the 21st century: Research, issues, and perspectives* (pp. 218–234). Springfield, IL: Charles C. Thomas.

Feagin, J. R. (2001). *Racist America: Roots, currents realities, & future reparation.* London: Routledge.

Fenning, P. & Rose, J. (2007). Overrepresentation of African American students in exclusionary discipline: The role of school policy. *Urban Education, 42*(6), 536–559.

Ferguson, A. A. (2001). *Bad boys: Public school in the making of Black masculinity.* Ann Arbor, MI: The University of Michigan Press.

Ferguson, R. F. (2007). *Toward excellence with equity: An emerging vision for closing the achievement* gap: Cambridge, MA: Harvard Education Press.

Ferguson, R. F. (2008). What we have learned about "stalled progress" in closing the Black–White achievement gap." In K. Magnuson & J. Waldfogel (Eds.), *Steady gains and stalled progress: Inequality and the Black-White test score gap.* New York: Russell Sage.

Fiedler, L. A. (1960). *Love and death in the American novel.* New York: Criterion.

Fletcher, M. A. (2007). The corner of progress and peril. In Staff of the Washington Post (Eds.), *Being a Black man: At the corner of progress and peril* (pp. 3–15). New York: Public Affairs.

Fordham, S. & Ogbu, J. U. (1986). Black students' school success: Coping with the "burden of acting white." *The Urban Review, 18*(3), 176–206.

Fordham, S. (1985). Black students' success: Coping with the "burden of acting white." (ERIC Document Reproduction Service No ED281948).

Freire, P. (1973). *Pedagogy of the oppressed*. New York: Seabury Press.

Freire, P. (2000). *Pedagogy of the oppressed*. New York: Continuum.

Fullan, M. (2001). *Leading in a culture of change*. San Francisco: Jossey-Bass.

Fullan, M. (2004). *Leading in a culture of change: Personal action guide and workbook*. San Francisco: Jossey-Bass.

Garrison-Wade, D., & Lewis, C. W. (2006). Tips for school principals and teachers: Helping Black students achieve. In J. L. Landsman & C. W. Lewis (Eds.), *White teachers/diverse classrooms: A guide to building inclusive schools, promoting high expectations, and eliminating racism* (pp. 150—161). Sterling, VA: Stylus.

Gause, C. P. (2005a). Guest editor's introduction: Edu-tainment: Popular culture in the making of schools for the 21st century. *Journal of School Leadership, 15*(3), 240–242.

Gause, C. P. (2005b). Navigating the stormy seas: Critical perspectives on the intersection of popular culture and educational leader-"ship." *Journal of School Leadership, 15*(3), 333–345.

George, N. (1998). *Hip hop America: Hip hop and the molding of Black generation x*. New York: Viking.

Geschwender, J. A. (1977). *Class, race, and worker insurgency: The league of revolutionary black workers*. Cambridge, MA: Cambridge University Press.

Gilligan, C. (1982). *In a different voice*. Cambridge, MA: Harvard University Press.

Gilroy, P. (1993). *The black Atlantic: Modernity and double consciousness*. Cambridge, MA: Harvard University Press.

Gines, K. T. (2005). Queen bees and big pimps: Sex and sexuality in hip hop. In D. Darby & T. Shelby (Eds.), *Hip hop and philosophy: Rhyme 2 reason*. Chicago, Illinois: Open Court.

Ginwright, S. A. (2004). *Black in school: Afrocentric reform, urban youth, and the promise of hip-hop culture*. New York: Teachers College Press.

Giroux, H. (1997). *Pedagogy and the politics of hope: Theory, culture, and schooling*. Boulder, CO: Westview.

Giroux, H. A. (1994). Doing cultural studies: Youth and the challenge of pedagogy. *Harvard Educational Review, 63*(3), 278–308.

Gladwell, M. (2000). *The tipping point: How little things can make a big difference*. New York: Back Bay Books.

Glaser, B. G. (1978). *Theoretical sensitivity: Advances in the methodology of grounded theory*. Mill Valley, CA: Sociology Press.

Glesne, C. (1999). *Becoming qualitative researchers: An introduction* (2nd ed.). New York: Longman.

Goodlad, J. I. (2004). Why we need public education. In C. Glickman (Ed.), *Letters to the next president: What we can do about the real crisis in public education* (pp. 54–60). New York: Teachers College Press.

Gordon, E. W. (2006) Establishing a system of public education in which all children achieve at high levels and reach their full potential. In T. Smiley (Ed.), *The covenant with Black America* (pp. 23–45). Chicago: Third World Press.

Gordan, L. (2005). Grown folks' business: The problem of maturity in hip hop. In D. Darby & T. Shelby (Eds.), *Hip hop and philosophy: Rhyme 2 reason,* (pp. 105–116). Chicago: Open Court.

Gorski, P. (2006). The unintentional undermining of multicultural education: Educators at the crossroads. In J. L. Landsman & C. W. Lewis (Eds.), *White teachers/diverse classrooms: A guide to building inclusive schools, promoting high expectations, and eliminating racism* (pp. 61–78). Sterling, VA: Stylus.

Gould, S. J. (1981). *The mismeasure of man.* New York: Norton.

Gregory, A., & Mosely, P. M. (2004). The discipline gap: Teachers' views on the over-representation of African American students in the discipline system. *Equity and Excellence in Education, 37*(1), 18–30.

Guy, T. C. (2004). Gangsta rap and adult education. *New Directions for Adult and Continuing Education, 101,* 43–57.

Haberman, M. (2005). Personnel Preparation and Urban schools. In F. E. Obiakor & F. D. Beachum (Eds.). *Urban education for the 21st century: Research issues and perspectives.* Springfield, Ill: Charles C. Thomas Publishers, LTD.

Hall, P. (1998). The relationship between types of rap memory in African American children. *Journal of Black Studies, 28*(6), 802–814.

Hall, S. (1992). Race, culture, and communications: Looking backward and forward at cultural studies. *Rethinking Marxism, 5,* 10–18.

Haller, E. J., & Kleine, P. F. (2001). *Using educational research: A school administrator's guide.* New York: Longman.

Hancock, S. D. (2006). White women's work: On the front lines of urban education. In J. Landsman & C. W. Lewis (Eds.), *White teachers/diverse classrooms: A guide to building inclusive schools, promoting high expectations, and eliminating racism* (pp. 93–109). Sterling, VA: Stylus.

Harney, W. (2001). Response to Skrla et al. The illusion of educational equity in Texas: A commentary on "accountability for equity." *International Journal of Leadership in Education, 4*(3), 267–275.

Harro, B. (2000). The cycle of socialization. In M. Adams, W. J. Blumenfield , R. Castaneda, H. W. Hackman, M. L. Peters, & X. Zuniga (Eds.), *Reading for diversity and social justice: An anthology on racism, anti-Semitism, sexism, heterosexism, ableism, classism,* (pp. 79–82). New York: Routledge.

Hill, M. L. (2009). *Beats, rhymes, and classroom life: Hip-hop pedagogy and the politics of identity.* New York: Teachers College Press.

hooks, b. (2003). Confronting class in the classroom. In A. Darder, M. Baltodano, & R. D.Torres (Eds.), *The critical pedagogy reader* (pp. 143–150). New York: Routledge.

hooks, b. (2004). *We real cool: Black men and masculinity.* New York: Routledge.

Hoy, W. K., & Miskel, C. G. (2005). *Educational administration: Theory, research, and practice* (7th ed.). Boston: McGraw-Hill.

Hu-DeHart, E. (2001). 21st-Century America: Black and White and Beyond. In C. Stokes, T. Melendez, and G. Rhodes-Reed (Eds.), *Race in the 21st Century America* (pp. 79–98). East Lansing, Michigan: Michigan State University Press.

Hunter, R. C., & Bartee, R. (2003). The achievement gap: Issues of competition, class, and race. *Education and Urban Society, 35*(2), 151–160.

Irvine, J. J. (2003*). Educating teachers for diversity: Seeing with a cultural eye.* New York: Teachers College Press.

Jackson, J. H. (2008). *Given half a chance: The Schott 50-state report on public education and African American males.* Cambridge, MA: Schott Foundation for Public Education.

Jackson, K. (1996). *America is me: 170 fresh questions and answers on Black American history.* New York: Harper Perennial.

Jenkins, J. C. (1985) *The politics of insurgency: The farm workers movement in the 1960s.* New York: Columbia University Press.

Jordan, W. D. (1968). *White over Black: American attitudes toward the Negro 1550–1812.* Chapel Hill, NC: The University of North Carolina Press.

Jones, E. P. (2007). Introduction. In Staff of the Washington Post (Eds.), *Being a black man: At the corner of progress and peril* (pp. xi–xvi). New York: Public Affairs.

Kailin, J. (2002). *Antiracist education: From theory to practice.* New York: Rowan & Littlefield.

Karenga, M. (1989). *The African-American holiday of Kwanzaa: A celebration of family, community, and culture.* Los Angeles: University of Sankore.

Karp, S. (2002). Let them eat test. *Rethinking schools, 16,* 3–4.

Karpicke, H. & Murphy, M. E. (1996). Productive school culture: Principals working from the inside. *National Association of Secondary School Principals, 80,* 26–32.

Katz, J. (1995). Advertisement and the construction of violent white masculinity. In G. Dines and J. Humez (Eds.). *Gender, race and class in the media: A text reader.* Thousand Oaks, CA: SAGE Publications.

Katz, J. (2000). Pornography and men's consciousness. In M. Adams, W. J. Blumenfield, R. Castaneda, H. W. Hackman, M. L. Peters, X. Zuniga (Eds.), *Reading for diversity and social justice: An anthology on racism, anti-Semitism, sexism, heterosexism, ableism, and classism* (pp. 247—251). New York: Routledge.

Keesing, R. M. (1974). Theories of culture. *Annual Review of Anthropology, 3,* 73–97.

Keleher, T. (2000). Racial disparities related to school zero tolerance policies: Testimony to the U.S. Commission on Civil Rights. *Educational Resource Information Center (ERIC). ED454324,* 1–12.

Keyes, C. (2002). *Rap music and street consciousness.* Urbana, IL: University of Illinois Press.

King, C. S. (1987). *The words of Martin Luther King, Jr.* New York: Newmarket Press.

King, M. L. (1958). Who speaks for the South? *Liberation,* March 1958, pp. 13ff.

Kitwana, B. (2002). *The hip-hop generation: Young blacks and the crisis in African American culture.* New York: Basic Civitas Books.

Kozol, J. (1991). *Savage inequalities: Children in American schools.* New York: Harper Perennial.

Kozol, J. (2005). *The shame of the nation: The restoration of apartheid schooling in America.* New York: Crown Publishers.

Kunjufu, J. (1990). *Countering the conspiracy to destroy black boys* (vol. III). Chicago: African American Images.

Kunjufu, J. (1993). *Hip-hop vs. MAAT: A psycho/social analysis of values.* Chicago African American Images.

Kunjufu, J. (1994). *Countering the conspiracy to destroy black boys* (vol. IV). Chicago: African American Images.

Kunjufu, J. (1995). *Countering the conspiracy to destroy Black boys* (Vol. 4). Chicago: African American Images.

Kunjufu, J. (2001). *State of emergency: We must save African American males.* Chicago: African American Images.

Kunjufu, J. (2002). *Black students—Middle class teachers.* Chicago: African American Images.

Lacy, K. R. (2007). *Blue-chip Black: Race, class and status in the new Black middle class.* Berkeley: University of California Press.

Ladson-Billings, G. (1994). *The dreamkeepers: Successful teachers of African-American students.* San Francisco: Jossey-Bass.

Ladson-Billings, G. (1995). But that's just good teaching! The case for culturally relevant pedagogy. *Theory into Practice, 34(3),* 159–165.

Lakomski, G. (1984). On agency and structure: Pierre Bourdieu and Jean-Claud Passeron's theory of symbolic violence, *Curriculum Inquiry, 14*(2), 151–163.

Landsman, J. (2006). When truth and joy are at stake: Challenging the status quo in the high school English class. In J. L. Landsman & C. W. Lewis (Eds.), *White teachers/diverse classrooms: A guide to building inclusive schools, promoting high expectations, and eliminating racism* (pp. 221–233). Sterling, VA: Stylus.

Landsman, J., & Lewis, C. W. (Eds.) (2006). *White teachers/diverse classrooms: A guide to building inclusive schools, promoting high expectations, and eliminating racism.* Sterling, VA: Stylus.

Lopez, G. R. (2003). The (racially neutral) politics of education: A critical race theory perspective. *Educational Administration Quarterly*, 39(1), 69–94.

Loury, G. C. (2002). *The anatomy of racial inequality.* Cambridge, MA: Harvard University Press.

Lowi, T. (1977). *The politic of disorder.* New York: Basic Books.

Majors, R., & Billson, J. (1992). *Cool pose: The dilemmas of black manhood in America.* New York: Touchtone.

Marble, M. (1993, October). Education and the premise of equality. *Jackson Advocate, 56*(3), 5A.

Massey, D., & Denton, N. (1993). *American apartheid: Segregation and the making of the underclass*. Cambridge, MA: Harvard University Press.

McCall, N. (1997). *What's going on*. New York: Random House.

McCray, C. R. (2008). Constructing a positive intrasection of race and class for the 21st Century. *Journal of School Leadership, 18*(2), 249–267.

McCray, C. R. Wright, J. V., & Beachum, F. D. (2004). Analysis of principals' perceptions of multicultural education. *Education, 125*(1), 111–120.

McCray, C. R., Alston, J. A., & Beachum, F. D. (2006). Principals' perceptions of multicultural education and school climate. *Multicultural Learning and Teaching, 1*(1), 12–22. Available: http://www.mltonline.org/current-articles/beachum2.pdf

McCray, C. R., & Beachum, F. D. (2006). A critique of zero tolerance policies: An issue of justice and caring. *Values and Ethics in Educational Administration, 5*(1), 1–8. Available: http://www.ed.psu.edu/UCEACSLE/VEEA/VEEA_Vol5Num1.pdf

McCray, C. R. Wright, J. V., & Beachum, F. D. (2007). Beyond *Brown*: Examining the perplexing plight of African American principals. *Journal of Instructional Psychology, 34*(4), 247–255.

McDermott, R., Raley, J. D., & Seyer-Ochi, I. (2009). Race and class in a culture of risk. *Review of Research in Education, 33*, 101–116.

McKinsey & Company (2009, April). *The economic impact of the achievement gap in America's schools*. New York: Author.

McWhorter, J. H. (2001). *Losing the race: Self-sabotage in Black America*. New York: Harper Perennial.

Mickel, E., & Mickel, C. (2002). Family therapy in transition: Choice theory and music. *International Journal of reality therapy, 21*, 37–40.

Milner, H. R. (2006). But good intentions are not enough: Theoretical and philosophical relevance in teaching students of color. In J. Landsman & C. W. Lewis (Eds.), *White teachers/diverse classrooms: A guide to building inclusive schools, promoting high expectations, and eliminating racism* (pp. 79–90). Sterling, VA: Stylus.

Mizialko, A. (2005). Reducing the power of "whiteness" in urban schools. In F. E. *Obiakor & F. D. Beachum (eds.), Urban education for the 21st century: Research, issues, and perspectives* (pp. 176–186). Springfield, IL: Charles C. Thomas.

Morrell, E., & Duncan-Andrade, J. M. R. (2002). Promoting academic literacy with urban youth through engaging in hip-hop culture. *English Journal, 91*(6), 88–92.

Mosca, F., & Hollister, A. (2004). External control and zero tolerance: Is fear of our youth driving these policies? *Educational Horizons, 83*(1), 2–5.

National Research Council, Committee on Minority Representation in Special Education (2002). In M. S. Donovan & C. T. Cross (Eds.). , *Minority students in special and gifted education*. Washington, DC: National Academy Press.

Neal-Barnett, A. M. (2001). Being black: A new conceptualization of acting white. In A. M. Neal-Barnett, J. Contreras, & K. Kerns (eds.), *Forging links: African American children clinical development perspective*. Westwood, CT: Greenwood Publishing Group.

Negy, C., Shreve, Jensen, B. J., & Uddin, N. (2003). Ethnic identity, self-esteem, and ethnocentrism: A study of social identity versus multicultural theory of development. *Cultural Diversity and Mental Health, 9*(4), 333–334.

Nieto, S. (2000). *Affirming diversity: The sociopolitical context of multicultural education* (3rd ed.). New York: Longman.

Nisbett, R. E. (2009). *Intelligence and how to get it: Why schools and cultures count.* New York: W. W. Norton & Company, Inc.

Noddings, N. (1992). *The challenge to care in schools: An alternate approach to education.* New York: Teachers College Press.

Noguera, P. (2003). *City schools and the American Dream: Reclaiming the promise of public education.* New York: Teachers College Press.

Noguera, P. A. (2004). Going beyond the slogans and rhetoric. In C. Glickman (Ed.), *Letters to the next president: What we can do about the real crisis in public education* (pp. 174–183). New York: Teachers College Press.

North, C. (2006). More than words? Delving into the substantive meaning(s) of "social justice" in education. *Review of Educational Research, 76*(4), 507–535.

O'Connor, C. (1997). Disposition towards (collective) struggle and educational resistance in the inner city: A case analysis of six African-American high schools students. *Educational Research Journal, 34*(4), 593–629.

O'Connor, C., Hill, L, D., & Robinson, S. R. (2009). Who's at risk in school and what's race got to do with it? *Review of Research in Education, 33,* 1–34.

Obiakor, F. E. (2001). *It even happens in "good" schools: Responding to culturally diversity in today's classrooms.* Thousand Oaks, CA: Corwin Press.

Obiakor, F. E. (2007). *Multicultural special education: Culturally responsive teaching.* Upper Saddle River, NJ: Pearson Merill/Prentice Hall.

Obiakor, F. E. (2008). *The eight-step approach to multicultural learning and teaching* (3rd ed.). Dubuque, IA: Kendall/Hunt.

Obiakor, F. E. (2009, October). *In search of equity, excellence, and access: Using the comprehensive support model to close the achievement gaps.* Keynote address at the "Closing the Achievement Gap" Conference, School of Education, Dominican University, River Forest, IL.

Obiakor, F. E., & Beachum, F. D. (2005a). Developing self-empowerment in African–American students using the comprehensive support model. *The Journal of Negro Education, 74*(1), 18–29.

Obiakor, F. E., & Beachum, F. D. (2005b). Urban education: The quest for democracy, equity, and excellence. In F. E. Obiakor & F. D. Beachum (Eds.), *Urban education for the 21st century: Research, issues, and perspectives* (pp. 3–19). Springfield, IL: Charles C. Thomas.

Ogbu, J. U. (2003). *Black American students in affluent suburb: A study of academic disengagement.* New Jersey: Lawrence Erlbaum.

Ogbu, J. (2004). Collective identity and the burden of 'acting white' in Black history and community, and education. *The Urban Review, 36*(1), 1–35.

Parrish, T. (2002). Racial disparities in the identification, funding, and provision of special education. In D. J. Losen & G. Orfield (Eds.), *Racial inequity in special education* (pp. 15–37) Cambridge, MA: Harvard Civil Rights Project.

Patterson, O. (2006). A poverty state of mind. *New York Times*. Retrieved September 22, 2009 from://www.nytimes.com/2006/03/26/opinion/26patterson.html.

Patton, P. L. (1998). The gangstas in our midst. *The Urban Review, 30*(1), 49–76.

Pawlas, G. E. (1997). Vision and school culture. *National Association of Secondary School Principals, 81*(587), 118–120.

Perry, T. (2003). Up from the parched earth: Toward a theory of African-American achievement. In T. Perry, C. Steel, & A. G. Hilliard (Eds.), *Young gifted and Black: Promoting high achieving among African-American students* (pp. 1–108). Boston: Beacon.

Perry, T., Steele, C., & Hilliard, A. (2003). *Young, Gifted, and Black: Promoting high achievement among African-American students*. Boston: Beacon Press.

Petchauer, E. (2009). Framing and reviewing hip-hop educational research. *Review of Educational Research, 79*(2), 946–978.

Peterson, R. L. (2003). Teaching the social curriculum: School discipline as instruction. *Preventing school failure, 47*(2), 66–73.

Pettit, B., & Western, B. (2004). Mass imprisonment and the life course: Race and class inequality in U.S. incarceration. *American Sociological Review, 69*, 151–169.

Powell, K. (2003). *Who's gonna take the weight?: Manhood, race, and power in America*. New York: Three Rivers Press.

Quarles, B. (1987). *The Negro in the making of America*. New York: Macmillan Publishing Company.

Raffaele-Mendez, L. M., Knoff, H. M., & Ferron, J.M. (2002). School demographics variables and out-of-school suspension rates: A quantitative and qualitative analysis of a large, ethnically diverse school district. *Psychology in the schools, 39*(3), 259–277.

Ripley, A. (2001). Throwing the book at kids. *Time, 157* (11), 34.

Rose, T. (1994). *Black noise: Rap music and Black culture in contemporary America*. Hanover, CT; Wesleyan University Press.

Rosenthal, R., & Jacobson, L. (1968). *Pygmalion in the classroom: Teachers expectation and pupils' intellectual development*. New York: Holt, Rinehart and Winston.

Rothenberg, P. (1998). *Race, class, and gender in the United State: An integrated Study*. (4th ed.). New York: St. Martin's Press.

Rothstein, S. W. (1996). *Schools and society: New perspectives in American education*. Englewood Cliffs, NJ: Prentice Hall.

Ryan, J. (2006). *Inclusive leadership*. San Francisco: Jossey-Bass.

Shelby, T. (2005). *We who are dark: The Philosophical foundations of black solidarity*. Cambridge, MA: The Belknap Press of Harvard University Press.

Shipler, D. K. (1997). *A country of strangers: Blacks and whites in America*. New York: Alfred A. Knopf.

Shusterman, R. (2005). Rap aesthetics: Violence and the art of keeping it real. In D.

Darby & T. Shelby (Eds.), *Hip hop and philosophy: Rhyme 2 reason*. Chicago, Illinois: Open Court.

Skiba, R. J., & Knesting, K. (2001). Zero tolerance, zero evidence: An analysis of school disciplinary practice . *New Directions for Youth Development, 92*, 17–43.

Skiba, R. J., & Peterson, R. L. (1999). Zap zero tolerance. *The education digest, 64*(8), 24–30.

Skiba, R. J., Michael, R. S., Nardo, A. C., & Peterson, R. L. (2002). The color of discipline: Sources of racial and gender disproportionality in school punishment. *Urban Review, 34*(4), 317–342.

Skiba, R. J., & Peterson, R. L. (1999). Zap zero tolerance. *The education digest, 64*(8), 24–30.

Skiba, R. J., Poloni-Staudinger, L., Gallini, S., Simmons, A. B., & Feggins-Azziz, L. R. (2007). Disparate access: The disproportionality of African American students with disabilities across educational environments. *Exceptional Children, 72(4)*, 411–424.

Skrla, L., Scheurich, J. J., Garcia, J., & Nolly, G. (2004). Equity audits: A practical leadership tool for developing equitable and excellent schools. *Educational Administration Quarterly, 40*(1), 133–161.

Smith, R., & Sapp, M. (2005). Insights into educational psychology: What urban school practitioners must know. In F. E. Obiakor & F. D. Beachum (Eds.), *Urban education for the 21st century: Research, issues, and perspectives* (pp. 100–113). Springfield, IL: Charles C. Thomas.

Solorzano, D. G. (1997). Images and words that wound: Critical race theory, racial stereotyping, and teacher education. *Teacher Education Quarterly, 24*(3), 5–19.

Spencer, M. B., Nollm, E., Stoltzfus, J., & Harpalani, V. (2001). Identity and school adjustment: Revisiting the "acting white" assumption. *Educational Psychologist, 36*(1), 1532–6985.

Starrat, R. J. (1991). Building an ethical school: A theory for practice in educational leadership. *Education Administration Quarterly, 27*(2), 185–202.

Starrat, R. J. (2004). *Ethical leadership*. San Francisco: Jossey Bass.

Stevenson, H. C. (1997). Managing anger: Protective, proactive, or adaptive racial socialization identity profiles and African-American manhood development. *Journal of Prevention and Intervention in the Community, 16*(1/2), 35–61.

Stewart, P. (2004). Who's playin' whom? Overwhelming influence of hip hop culture, rap, music on HBCU campuses concerns students, faculty. *Black Issues in Higher education*, April 22.

Strauss, A. L., & Corbin, J. (1998). *Basics of qualitative research: Techniques and procedures for developing grounded theory*. Thousand Oaks, CA: Sage.

Strayhorn, T. (2008). The role of supportive relationships in facilitating African American males' success in college. *NASPA Journal, 45*(1), 26–48.

Stuckey, S. (1987). *Slave culture: Nationalist theory & the foundations of Black America*. New York: Oxford University Press.

Tatum, B. D. (1997). *Why are all the Black kids sitting together in the cafeteria?: And other conversations about race*. New York: Basic Books.

Tatum, B. D. (2007). *Can we talk about race? And other conversations in an era of school reseg-regation*. Boston: Beacon Press.

Taylor, P. C. (2005). Does hip hop belong to me? The philosophy of race and culture. In D. Darby & T. Shelby (Eds.), *Hip hop and philosophy: Rhyme 2 reason*. Chicago: Open Court.

Thomas, D. E., & Stevenson, H. (2009). Gender risks and education: The particular classroom challenges for urban low-income African American boys. *Review of Research in Education, 33*, 160–180.

Thompson III, T. L. (2007). Historical and contemporary dilemmas facing urban Black male students today: Focusing on the past to correct present and future deficits. In M. C. Brown & R. D. Bartee (Eds.). *Still not equal: Expanding educational opportunity in society* (pp. 49—63). New York: Peter Lang.

Thompson, R. F. (1996). Hip-hop 101. In W. E. Perkins (Ed.), *Droppin' science: Critical essays on rap music and hip-hop culture* (pp. 211–219). Philadelphia: Temple University Press.

Thrasher, J. F., Niederdeppe, J. D., Jackson, C., & Farrelly, M. C. (2006). Using anti-tobacco industry messages to prevent smoking among high-risk adolescents. *Health Education Research, 21*(3), 325–337.

Tillman, L. C. (2006). Researching and writing from an African-American perspective: Reflective notes on three research studies. *International Journal of Qualitative Studies in Education, 19*(3), 265–287.

Took, K. J., & Weiss, D. S. (1994). The relationship between heavy metal and rap music on adolescent turmoil: Real or artifact? In *Adolescence, 29*, 613–621.

Tyson, E. H. (2002). Hip hop therapy: An exploratory study of rap music intervention with at-risk and delinquent youth. *Journal of Poetry Therapy, 15*(3), 131–144.

Tyson, K., Darity, W., & Castellino, D. R. (2005). It's not "a Black thing": Understanding the burden of acting white and other dilemmas of high achievement. *American Sociological Review, 70*(4), 582–605.

U.S. Department of Education. (1999). Projected student suspension rates values for the nation's public schools by race/ethnicity: Elementary and secondary school civil rights compliance report. Washington D. C.: Office of Civil Rights.

Vance, B. (2001). *From ghetto to community: The resurrection of African American institutions*. Chicago: African American Images.

Venkatesh, E. A. (2006). *Off the Books: The underground economy of the urban poor*. Cambridge, MA: Harvard University Press.

Villegas, A. M., & Lucas, T. (2002). *Educating culturally responsive teachers: A coherent approach*. Albany, NY: State University of New York Press.

Wacquant, L. (1998). A Black city within the White: Revisiting America's dark ghetto. *Black Renaissance—Renaissance Noire, 2*(1), 141–151.

Wacquant, L. (2000). The new 'peculiar institution': On the prison as surrogate ghetto. *Theoretical Criminology, 4*(3), 377–389.

Wacquant, L. (2001). Deadly symbiosis: When ghetto and prison meet and mesh. *Punishment and Society, 3*(1), 95–134.

Wacquant, L. (2002). From slavery to mass incarceration: Rethinking the 'race question' in the U.S. *New Left Review,* 13, 41–60.

Wagner, T. (2001). Leadership for learning: An action theory of school change. *Phi Delta Kappan, 82*(5), 378–383.

Wagner, T. (2008). *The global achievement gap: Why even our best schools don't teach the new survival skills our children need—And what we can do about it.* New York: Peruses Publishing.

Walker, V. S., & Snarey, J. R. (2004). Race matters in moral formation. In V. S. Walker & J. R. Snarey (Eds.), *Race-ing moral formation: African American perspectives on care and justice* (pp. 1–22). New York: Teachers College Press.

Warikoo, N, & Carter, P. (2009). Cultural explanations for racial and ethnic stratification in academic achievement: A call for a new improved theory. *Review of Educational Research, 79*(1), 366–394.

Watkins, W. H. (2004, July). *Leadership, culture, and schooling.* Unpublished draft presented at the Fourth Annual Education Summit Conference on Leadership, Culture and Schooling, Miami University, Oxford, OH.

West, C. (1993). *Race matters.* New York: Vintage Books

West, C. (1994). *Race matters.* New York: Vintage Books.

West, C. (2004). *Democracy matters: Winning the fight against imperialism.* New York: Penguin Press.

West , C. (2008). *Hope on a tightrope: Words and wisdom.* Carlsbad, CA: Hay House, Inc.

White, J. L. & Cones III, J. H. (1999). *Black man emerging: Facing the past and seizing a future in America.* New York: W. H. Freeman and Company.

Wilson, A. (1990). *Black on black violence.* New York: African World Info Systems.

Wilson, W. J. (2004). *Race, class, and the postindustrial city: William Julius Wilson and the promise of sociology/ Edition 1.* Albany, NY: State University of New York Press.

Wilson, W. J. (2009). *More than just race: Being Black and poor in the inner city.* New York: W.W. Norton & Company.

Wood, P. H. (1974). *Black majority: Negroes in colonial South Carolina from 1670 through the Stono Rebellion.* New York: W. W. Norton & Company.

Woodward, C. V. (1974). *The strange career of Jim Crow* (3rd ed.). New York: Oxford University Press.

Yeo, F., & Kanpol, B. (1999). Introduction: Our own "Peculiar Institution": Urban education in 20th-century America. In F. Yeo & B. Kanpol (Eds.), *From nihilism to possibility: Democratic transformations for the inner city* (pp. 1–14). Cresskill, NJ: Hampton Press, Inc.

Young, I. M. (1990). *Justice and the politics of difference.* Princeton University Press.

Index

Educational PSYCHOLOGY

Critical Pedagogical Perspectives

Greg S. Goodman, *General Editor*

Educational Psychology: Critical Pedagogical Perspectives is a series of relevant and dynamic works by scholars and practitioners of critical pedagogy, critical constructivism, and educational psychology. Reflecting a multitude of social, political, and intellectual developments prompted by the mentor Paulo Freire, books in the series enliven the educator's process with theory and practice that promote personal agency, social justice, and academic achievement. Often countering the dominant discourse with provocative and yet practical alternatives, *Educational Psychology: Critical Pedagogical Perspectives* speaks to educators on the forefront of social change and those who champion social justice.

For further information about the series and submitting manuscripts, please contact:

> Dr. Greg S. Goodman
> Department of Education
> Clarion University
> Clarion, Pennsylvania
> *ggoodman@clarion.edu*

To order other books in this series, please contact our Customer Service Department at:

> (800) 770-LANG (within the U.S.)
> (212) 647-7706 (outside the U.S.)
> (212) 647-7707 FAX

Or browse online by series at:

> www.peterlang.com